Small Business Sucks

...but it doesn't have to

by Paul Thompson

Copyright © 2000 by Paul Thompson

All rights reserved. No part of this publication may be reproduced, stored in a retrieval system, or transmitted, in any form or by any means, electronic, mechanical, photocopying, recording, or otherwise, without the written prior permission of the author.

Illustrations: Shawn O'Connor
Cover Design and Layout: Geoff Gosson

Printed in Canada

```
Canadian Cataloguing in Publication Data

Thompson, Paul
   Small business sucks-- but it doesn't have to




   ISBN 1-55212-392-8

   1. Small business--Management.  2. Small business--Humor.  I. Title.
HD62.7.T46 2000                     658.02'2                 C00-910506-9
```

TRAFFORD

This book was published *on-demand* **in cooperation with Trafford Publishing.**
On-demand publishing is a unique process and service of making a book available for retail sale to the public taking advantage of on-demand manufacturing and Internet marketing.
On-demand publishing includes promotions, retail sales, manufacturing, order fulfilment, accounting and collecting royalties on behalf of the author.

Suite 6E, 2333 Government St., Victoria, B.C. V8T 4P4, CANADA
Phone   250-383-6864   Toll-free   1-888-232-4444 (Canada & US)
Fax   250-383-6804   E-mail   sales@trafford.com
Web site www.trafford.com   TRAFFORD PUBLISHING IS A DIVISION OF TRAFFORD HOLDINGS LTD.
Trafford Catalogue #00-0056   www.trafford.com/robots/00-0056.html

10   9   8   7   6   5   4   3   2   1

Acknowledgments

Gratitude courses through every fibre of my body. Along the way the following people have encouraged, prodded, poked and pushed (the '3P' factor) me to complete this work.

My brother Peter said to me, "*Paul - hear me on this,* **keep believing in yourself.** *Don't, I repeat, don't ever doubt yourself. It seems to me that the air around you is electric. What you can do is almost magical."*

Well it was with the help of all these people I have listed below (in no particular order) that self-doubt eased its way to self-confidence.

Thank you everybody, for all your love, help and support.

My dad, A.G. and my mom, Bubs, bless their souls, my wife, Susan, my son, Gavin, Josie the wonderdog, Michael Losier, Johanna Bates, Cynthia Woodward, Steve Charles, Felicity Adamthwaite, Linda Baynham, Georgia Nichols, Mary Eschenko, Dyan Grant-Francis, Geoff Gosson, Darlene Gunter, Paul MacDonald, Lindsay Grover, Tanis Toope, Bruce Batchelor, Gail Patterson, Scooter the cat, Chuck Baynham and the ever-present Carole Matthews.

Preface

People from every profession contribute to the fabric of our society. The small businessperson lives in each and every one of us. Whether our experience is the lemonade stand when we were young or the running of a store, bed and breakfast, office, or whatever detail our dreams took as we matured, the thread of small business has been woven deeply into our collective psyche.

The entrepreneurial spirit includes everyone who has ever had a craft table, or sold any one of a number of home marketing products. This spirit flows in the successful business people who now have a chain of many stores.

This book, **Small Business Sucks™**, is a light-hearted approach to the age-old problems that appear in small business every day. It pokes fun at our vocabulary. It illustrates things that surround our business day. It illuminates for many, terms that are thought to be understood but are often shades of grey in a world dominated by black and white. You read the 'Glossary' as you would a dictionary except the terms are by order of importance. The first word then, under A, is RENT, because for the small business person rent is first

The stories in the 'Slice of Life' Section mirror and reflect the episodes that easily could have happened in the lives of most people. We all can all see ourselves as the hero, the heroine, the villain or maybe all three. The value in this work for both the 'Glossary' and 'Slice of Life' is that upon reading it's contents, some chord might resonate with the reader. Something might enable the individual not to take themselves or others so seriously. The ability of seeing others in a different light might occur. Readers might be motivated to laugh or chuckle at themselves. There might be a chance of a deeper sense of understanding and appreciation for the trials and tribulations that are involved for everyone in small business.

Landlords, bankers, merchants, and professionals might see themselves in these pages. Who knows perhaps they all could really talk and listen to one another.

While the title of this book is **Small Business Sucks**™, the thrust of this work is that it certainly doesn't have to suck. Hopefully, through some of the fun and instructive nudgings in this book, business people, their families and friends can find play value, a bit of instruction and discover some new skills to continue making small business happen!

THE
GLOSSARY

terms in order of importance

A

Rent 19
Accountant 20
Triple Net 25
Monthly Take Off Figures 27

B

Freeze 29
Rent Distress 30
Myopia 30
Utilities 31

C

Collection Agency 32
Lawyer 34
Cash Flow 36

D

Loop 38
DBA 39

E

Notice of Default 39
Bailiff 40

Bank Accounts 41
Bank Charges 42
Discount Rate 46
Credit Card 47
Indentured Slavery 48

F

Landlord 49
Landlord's Agent 50
Management Co. 50
Site Manager 50
Neophytes 51
Fear 53
Fun 54
Pencil Case 54

G

Gatekeepers 57

H

Heads Up 59

I

Employment Insurance Commission 60
Insurance 62

J

Suicide 63
Being in Action 64

K

Support Team 65
Professional Development 66

L

Kindness 69
Inc., Ltd. 69
Ministry of Labour 70

M

Capital 73
Capital Expenditure 74
Capital Gain 74
GSA 75
Balance Sheet 76

N

NSF 76
Advertising 77
Moniker 80

O

Staff Meetings 81
Boss's Bundt Cake 84

P

Game Face 86
Karma 89

Q

Quarters 90
Attitude 91
Commitment 92
Faith 94
Integrity 94
Trust 95
Communication 96

R

End of the Day Routine 97
Start of the Day Routine 97
Trend 98
Relli 99
Lineupee 99

S

Shares/Assets 101
Shareholder's Loan 102
Director 102
Responsibilities 103
Sales Rep 104
Profit Margin 105
Terms 106

T

Under the Table 108
Reconciliation 109
Statement of Account 109
Debit Card 111
Trustee in Bankruptcy 115

U

Conditional Surrender 116
Petty Cash 117

V

Guts 118
Bank Communication 119
Voice Mail 120

W

Wholesale/Retail 123
Write Off 125
Mark Up 126
Book Value 127
Wiz 127

X

Xenogasaphobia 128
Variable 128
Plan 129

Y

Yurt 135
Canada/USA Comparison 136
Boundaries 137

Z

Trial Balance 140
Asset 140
Job 141
Juggling 141
Ziggurat 142

THE
GLOSSARY

terms in alphabetical order

A

Accountant 20
Advertising 77
Asset 140
Attitude 91

B

Bailiff 40
Bank Accounts 41
Bank Charges 42
Bank Communication 119
Balance Sheet 76
Being in Action 64
Book Value 127
Boundaries 137
Boss's Bundt Cake 84

C

Canada/USA Comparison 136
Capital 73
Capital Expenditure 74
Capital Gain 74
Cash Flow 36

Collection Agency 32

Commitment 92
Communication 96
Conditional Surrender 116
Credit Card 47

D

DBA 39
Debit Card 111
Default 39
Director 102
Discount Rate 46

E

Employment Insurance Commission 60
End of the Day Routine 97

F

Faith 94
Fear 53
Freeze 29
Fun 54

G

Game Face 86
Gatekeepers 57

GSA 75
Guts 118

H

Heads Up 59

I

Inc., Ltd. 69
Indentured Slavery 48
Insurance 62
Integrity 94

J

Job 141
Juggling 141

K

Karma 89
Kindness 69

L

Landlord 49
Landlord's Agent 50
Lawyer 34
Loop 38

Lineupee 99

M

Management Company 50
Mark Up 126
Ministry of Labour 70
Moniker 80
Monthly Take-Off-Figures 27
Myopia 30

N

Neophytes 51
Notice of Default 39
NSF 76

P

Pencil Case 54
Petty Cash 117
Plan 129
Professional Development 66
Profit Margin 105

Q

Quarters 90

R

Reconciliation 109
Relli 99
Rent 19
Rent Distress 30
Responsibilities 103

S

Sales Rep 104
Site Manager 50
Shares/Assets 101
Shareholder's Loan 102
Staff Meetings 81
Start of the Day Routine 97
Statement of Account 109
Suicide 63
Support Team 65

T

Terms 106
Trial Balance 140
Trend 98
Triple Net 25
Trust 95
Trustee in Bankruptcy 115

U

Under the Table 105
Utilities 31

V

Variable 128
Voice Mail 120

W

Wholesale/Retail 123
Wiz 127
Write Off 125

X

Xenogasaphobia 128

Y

Yurt 135

Z

Ziggurat 142

A SLICE OF LIFE

Our Lady of the Melon 146
Adopting the Neighbourhood 150
Memories 153
Life & Art 156
Work Ethic 158
Family Business and the Family 159
The Dedicated Employee 163
Irreplaceable 166
Workplace Demeanor 168
Why I Can't Come to Work 171
WANTED 174
Relative Worker Story #309 177
Relative Worker Story #310 178
The Rellis are Coming! 179
Coffee Stores 181
The Customer is Always Right 182
The Frequent Shopper 183
My Life Revolves Around Me 185
Who's Right? 188
How Much Did They Spend? 191
Request #335443 193
The Nuts and Bolts 194
The End and 195

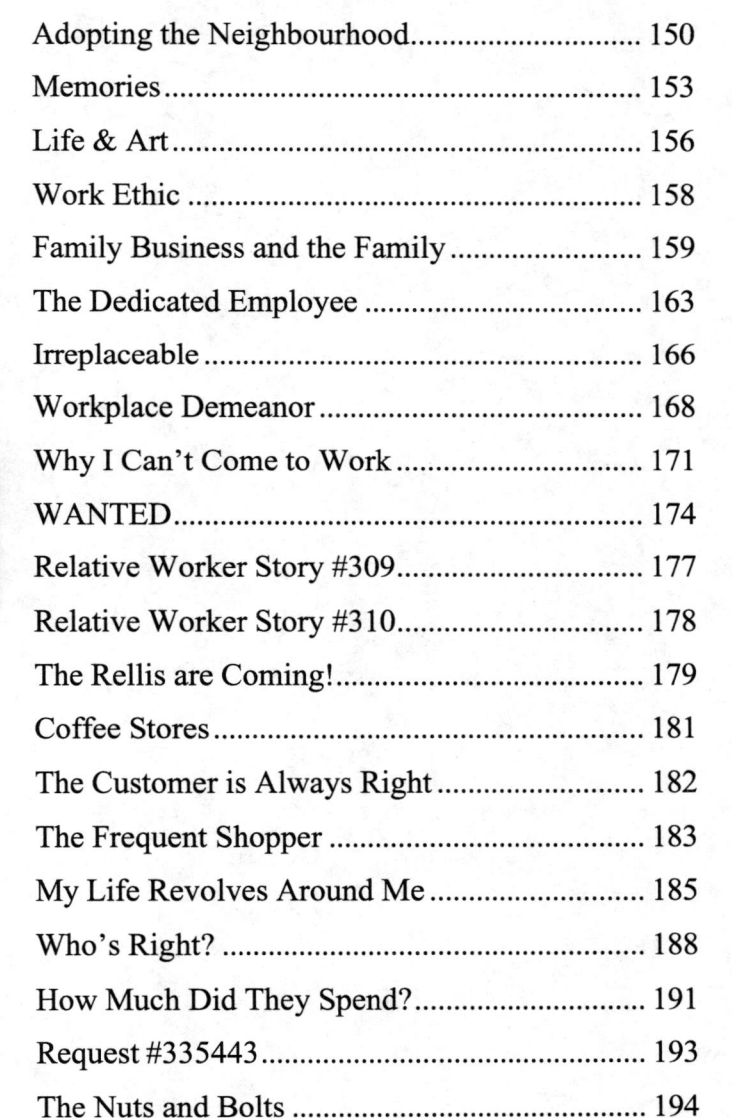

Terms
in order of importance

RENT

This is a term for small business people.

Rent is money that you have agreed to pay to someone else to make him or her wealthy. Rent is the amount of money you have agreed to pay to your landlord on the first of each month. It is not due until the seventh of the month.

You can possibly make weekly installments of your rent when cash flow is tight, with the consent of the landlord. You are fulfilling your part of the bargain by having the intent to pay.

If you have a payroll and the rent due on the same day, guess what? Pay the payroll and hold the rent cheque.

ACCOUNTANT

This is a descriptor noun.

This term describes people who are skilled at 1 8 7 2 3 7 2 3 8 7 1 8 7 3 8 2 7 3 8 7 1 8 7 3 8 7 2 3 8 7 2 8 3 7 8 2 7 3 8 7 2 3 8 7 2 1 8 4 7 5 0 2 5 5 7 7 4 0 4 4 4 5 9 5 8 5 8 9 5 9 8 9 5 8 9 4 8 5 9 0 7 5 7 5 4 5 9 8 5 8 5 8 4 9 5 8 0 3 8 5 9 4 8 5 9 4 8 5 9 4 8 5 9 4 8 5 9 8 4 9 5 8 4 9 8 5 9 4 8 5 9 8 4 9 5 8 3 0 4 9 5 8 0 9 4 5 8's.

Or so they think. Unless they are equally skilled at communication, you are instantly in trouble.

Here are some guidelines that might help you avoid costly (read it will cost you money in the short run) and expensive mistakes (read it could cost you your company and your personal financial fortune and future).

Always meet the accountant first and grill them for an hour at no charge to you. Be sure to ask them:
- How much an hour it is for them to work for you?
- What will they accomplish for you?
- How do they count their hours?
- How do they want to be paid?
- Are there any hidden charges?
- Who is responsible for GST, PST, and other tax reporting?

- Who is responsible for Revenue Canada and corporate tax filing?
- Who is responsible for your personal tax preparation and filing?
- Who does the work for the year-end review?
- **How much will this cost?**
- Ask who retains the file if there is a dispute.
- Demand that you have sole access to your file at all times whether or not you are current with the money they claim you owe.
- Request a retainer letter from them with all of the above in writing.

Point of Interest

The following are accounting stories. If you have one to match, write us so it may be included in my sequel.

A small business was bought in a small city and, of course, an accountant was recommended. Since someone else had recommended the same firm, the new owners, Bob and Cindy, happily entered into an arrangement with the company we shall call Company #1.

Partners, Gerald and Gertrude Accountants, were chosen based on the above recommendations. Our new business owners chose Gertrude who appeared to be a bright young woman with a flare for figures. **Just what they needed!**

Bob and Cindy asked none of the previous questions.

The accountant immediately wanted to establish a charge account at the family business. Of course, why not? Time passes and the company has moderate success. The accountant praises the management style and the books including the ledger of this family business. Indeed, they were the finest set of books in the entire city. **The owners were pleased.**

When year end came, they were charged extra money to have their year end prepared. The accountant and the owners declared a $13,000.00 bonus. Bob, the baffled owner said, *"how so, there is no money in the bank account."*

"Well it is just figures and its only on paper. By the way, if you are short of money, just cash some of your RRSPs and inject the money as a shareholder's loan", said Gertrude, the bright accountant.

The accountants, Gerald and Gertrude, had a huge fight. The fallout resulted in the breakup of the firm. Bob and Cindy our erstwhile owners were transferred to a new firm, Company # 2 with Gertrude in charge of this firm.

Things were muddling along. The books were still praised by the accountant. Costs were going up. A meeting with the bank and the accountant failed to impress the financial institution as to how well this company was doing. A loan and or line of credit was denied. A huge bill was issued to the owners including bookkeeping. ***Did you catch that?***

Bob questioned all these new charges including a telephone call on such-and-such a date. In Bob's journal Gertrude called him to ask him a question. Now they're all fighting. The accountant's charge account is closed and the owner's bill escalates. In the accountant's office the question Bob asked was, *"how could there be a charge for bookkeeping - when you don't do that??!!"*

The bill was reduced by $1,000. Bob and Cindy land back at Gerald's company. **But the file remains the property of Gertrude, the first accountant!**

The scenario is that to get Bob and Cindy up to date all the work has to be reinvented! That's right! The books, year-end and all the work Gertrude did has to be done again.

Gerald is a nice guy. He is always making jokes and smiling and laughing, showing what's new on the computer. The sad truth is that the work was not ready on time - the figures looked good but shades of reality were beginning to disappear. Things were missed. Gerald issues the order to, *"go and get more money from your RRSPs."* (It was as though he forgot the counting part of accounting, and he had rarely heard the word accountable.)

A new wrinkle was added. Gerald sold his company to another accounting firm. As you have probably already guessed, the owner's file was part of the assets of the firm. Now they are with Company #3

You also guessed it. This new company said everything was wrong (Bob and Cindy were beginning to realize that). Additionally, the fees were double that of Gerald the accountant.

So now what? Year end and taxes are now in a huge mess. Company #3 is trying to charge big bucks that this small business doesn't have. Remember they had to cash in all their RRSPs. Company #3 did admit that there were huge mistakes all along the way.

Enter Company #4. This company, for a monthly fee, would:
- Collect all your information in a prescribed format;
- Then they would analyze it and return it to you in the form of monthly statements, with national comparisons;
- All of this would funnel into a year end report;
- Which of course would be preceded by the 3 quarterly reports;
- Sounds like business doesn't it??

To contact this company for the nearest branch to you call Padgett Business Services, 1-800-PADGETT.

This is an international organization that caters solely to small and medium-sized businesses. They are fiscal wizards in a world of mediocrity.

TRIPLE NET
This is a term to confuse.

No, it's not three nets in one, nor is it three nets tied together. It is a term that the landlords and realtors bandy about as if every one knows exactly what it is.

Triple Net is all costs attributable to the premises including:
- Taxes;
- Insurance;
- Common area maintenance;
- Lighting;
- Janitorial services;
- Management fees;
- All fees that can be charged back to the space (your premises). The tenant is responsible for everything above base rent.

This is normally on a 'per square foot' basis and is proportionate in nature.

The question for this term is: *"What are the triple net charges for this space?"*

For example, a 1,000 square foot space is leased @ $24.00 per square foot, per month. However, a company leasing the premises must pay a monthly total of $3,300.00. The difference is $9.00 extra per square foot per month! Then the triple net charge is $9.00 per square foot, per month.

A commercial real estate agent who deals in small and large business space rentals said, *"that out of every hundred people who are renting space only nine would recognize it, be able to explain what triple net is, and how it impacts on their rent."* The greater horror is in asking the question: How does the tenant recoup the 'per square foot' cost so that their profit margin keeps them viable?

MONTHLY TAKE OFF FIGURES
This is generally mathematical fiction.

These are known in the business world as the monthlies. It takes about 5 to 15 days into the next the month to have these figures ready to see how you actually did in the last 30 days. The value of these figures is that they can show the decline and no growth scenario or the inch by inch improvement each month.

The following format will help you generate your own monthly figures.

Revenue
Under this heading list all the money that your company earns.

Expenses
List all the things that cost your company money. Include cost of goods sold, selling expenses, and payroll.

Net Income
This figure is arrived at by subtracting your expenses from your revenue. Everyone has seasonal highs and lows. Your first year establishes your base line from which you can measure your growth as a business and your profit picture.

FREEZE

*This is what the small businessperson feels like under the **freeze!***

FREEZE

This is a horror show.

This has nothing to do with the weather or something cold in your freezer, or the latest character in a Batman movie, or the temperature your relationship develops after one of you has done something stupid. It does however have something to do with your bank account and the banking laws in this country. The government of Canada, the provincial government and the various law courts can *freeze* your bank business account and take all the money to satisfy the unpaid taxes or a judgment order against your company.

RENT DISTRESS

This is a contractual clause in a lease.

This does not mean that your rent needs a counsellor or psychologist. It does however mean that your landlord has rent owed to him/her. It also means that he can now seek other means to collect said rent such as your friendly bailiff.

MYOPIA

This is a weakness.

This term applies to people who lack vision or have trouble seeing the picture with the same clarity as the person who has the vision. The visionary is generally the owner. However, the visionary is sometimes a gifted employee, a dedicated worker or the spouse of any of the above.

Myopia is the constant roadblock put in front of those who *want to make it work*.

Myopia is frequently found in financial institutions that claim they are only interested in the bottom line. They generally cannot see the bottom line for all the figures in front of it. Remember the saying, *"you can't see the forest for the trees?"* This is very applicable here.

The medical point of view gives up this definition for myopia...*short sighted*.

The advice here is:

When dealing with a financial institution ask them not to have myopia with you or your company...

UTILITIES
These are things you must have.

You can't do without things like electricity and the phone. These allow small businesses to communicate. Thank God for Alexander Graham Bell. Then there is Ben Franklin and Thomas Edison's gift to the small business community. It is strange that when both of these geniuses created their inventions, they didn't have a monopoly like the current holders of your electricity company, your gas company and the telephone company.

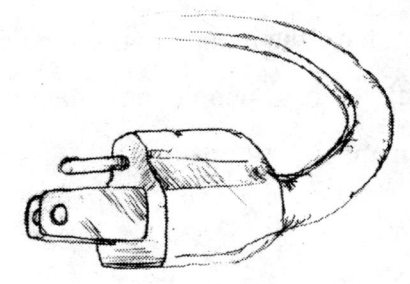

COLLECTION AGENCY

This is only a group of people.

This is a group of people who now have a third party debt.

Remember that...A THIRD PARTY DEBT. *Your* company is the third party. The people to whom your company owes money have waited the ninety days (or in some cases, years) for the money. They now have placed you in collection. The people to whom you owed the original money have lost a portion of the money. The collection agency charges them to collect the outstanding debt. The collection agents are paid commission.

The following are some tips on how to handle these sometimes ill-mannered and insolent and mostly rude individuals.

- Never spend the money and call back a long distance number. If you don't have the money to pay the money on the debt, you don't have the money to use long distance.
- Don't let these people intimidate you.
- Remember your position.

- You are an owner.
- These people are usually entry level, uneducated, anger-filled nobodies to whom you owe nothing. They are at best telemarketers and at worst, people with poor vocabularies.
- **They are not officers of any court**.
- They do not have any official designation or jurisdiction. They are clerks.
- The fact that they call themselves collection *officers* doesn't give them any legal or police-like powers.
- They will attempt to prey on your insecurities. Don't let them.
- Set the boundaries right away. You are the only one to whom financial information may be given. They cannot legally disclose information to any of your employees.
- Don't give out your home number or let your employees give out your home number.
- Do not promise anything. No matter how demanding, aggressive, pushy, bitchy, or *cunning* they may be.
- Don't be afraid to be honest with them. Tell them you have no money. It's the truth. Generally they don't like it, but they can't do a thing about it.
- Don't be afraid of threats of court action:
    - a) It gives you more time;
    - b) It erodes their profit factor;
    - c) It costs them money;
    - d) They rarely ever go to the trouble of going to court.

- Remember the golden rule. He who has the gold makes the rules. In this case you don't have any gold. That's why they're calling.
- Return their calls or information from a different telephone or, if it's an 800 number, call from a public telephone.
- Dial *67 to block your telephone number. Don't be afraid to hang up on them again and again.
- If they request that you courier or XpressPost anything, *don't unless they pay for it*. They won't!
- Don't let them embarrass you.
- Be as tough and aggressive with them as they are trying to be with you.
- For most of them, it is theater and generally THEY ARE PLAYING TO AN EMPTY HOUSE. In the real world they would never get the part.

LAWYER

This is the small businessperson's advocate.

Indeed the French term for lawyer is *un avocat*. One who advocates for your best interest sums up the most important feature of lawyers. These individuals are necessary for the survival of small business people. They can unwind things like leases, advise on matters pertaining to annual meetings and refer you to the appropriate individuals when you are in trouble.

Pick a firm with more than one lawyer on the team. You never know when you will need an expert in small business suits. I don't mean the suits you wear I mean lawsuits - the action where people are suing you and your company.

"People would sue?"

You bet, everyone from disgruntled employees to suppliers, to customers who have a differing opinion. Include the general public who have slipped, tripped, or chipped something or some part of themselves on or about your premises.

Legal advice can be obtained yearly by having your lawyer on a retainer which is a certain amount of money paid at the beginning of the year. To do large-scale work for you - anything from reading of the lease, counter-suing, protecting you from a lawsuit, to filing bankruptcy - a retainer must be paid to your lawyer before the work starts. At the conclusion of the legal service you will be invoiced for the balance owing.

Don't be afraid to ask how much an hour you are being charged, and whether the clock is ticking or not. Remember that the lawyer is working for you.

CASH FLOW

These words generally do not go together.

This is a term that bankers use. It is also a term that small businesses try to wrap their minds around. Now metaphorically, when you think of small business cash flow, think of Niagara Falls! You'll note our graphic image shows massive volumes of water going in only one direction. That is the general idea with small business cash flow. It is, however, instructive to note that events like Christmas or seasonal peaks for each business generate more than the daily cash grab. If the money generated is enough, stash some of it for those dog days of summer or your lowest month to help stretch your $$$$. Other clues to help with your cash flow are:

- Pay the 4% vacation pay to your staff each pay cheque.
- Establish a contingency fund. For example, start with $100 and add $100 monthly.
- Pay cash for everything.
- Pay the corporate credit card on time or hold it for an emergency.
- Don't accept debit cards (almost impossible) or pass the charge the bank charges you on to the consumer.
- Have minimum charges for the privilege of paying by credit card, or debit card. For example, the minimum direct debit charge will be $6.45. The minimum credit card transaction will be $10.45.

The seemingly endless flow of cash in only one direction.

LOOP

This is a figure made by a line crossing itself.

A loop is, in reality, what happens to small business when they try to pay back debt from current sales. They're in the loop because often (almost always) projections never equal fiscal reality. One prominent banker said, "*All sales projections are hot air.*" Though this person needed better skills in people management, he has proven to be correct nine times out of ten.

Most small businesses in Canada are in the loop.

DBA

This is a secret code.

This is the designation for 'doing business as.' For example, if your limited or incorporated company is a numbered company it can do business as ABC Book Store, a Division of 3458 Ont. Ltd.

NOTICE OF DEFAULT

This is a contractual term in a lease.

NO, it not your fault, it's DEFAULT! This is a letter your landlord will send you when you have not paid your rent. It is the heads up (see HEADS UP) that you need to have a conversation with the landlord's agent, the landlord's management company, or the site manager. It is also the heads up that the landlord can send in a bailiff to secure the assets of the company to meet the rent. Yes, they can lock the door and sell off your computer, your lunch, your leasehold improvements, the pictures of your children, your stock, etc.

Make sure that if you are in this position, you don't have sufficient assets in the store to satisfy this requirement. If you are in this position, you need to be talking to your lawyer, and possibly a trustee in bankruptcy (or attempting to pull a midnight move).

BAILIFF

This is a licensed and bonded individual.

Unlike the 'collections officer,' this person is empowered. He or she is authorized to seize goods and chattels (that means your equipment, stock, even perishables like food if it's a restaurant), leasehold improvements like marble counters and walls, delivery vans and anything else you can think of.

They are sanctioned by the Attorney General's office of each province. They can enforce the awarding (that means *take*) of company's possessions to a creditor from a court action (that means someone suing you). In the case of the government, you don't even have to be notified of the action.

BANK ACCOUNTS

These are necessary tools.

There are in fact many types of bank accounts for the small businessperson. For the retailer or small business that is incorporated there is the Bank of Record. That is the bank registered at your lawyer's office as your official company bank.

Then there is the VISA or MASTERCARD account that you must have at one of the opposing banks. This account will receive the deposits from the purchases that people make using VISA or MASTERCARD.

There should be accounts for the taxes you collect for GST, PST and items like source deductions, employment insurance and the Worker's Compensation Board. *Why???*

BECAUSE, as a business you collect money that does not belong to you. For example the net total at the end of the day in the daily ring off, includes money that belongs first to the federal government as GST. It is not your money to use for cash flow, rent, wages or anything else.

For the practitioner, consultant, doctor, or home office person there should still be a separate bank account into which all money made by the "company" will be deposited. Then if you have to write yourself a cheque for the mortgage, food, the car insurance, or whatever, you can do it after you pay yourself and take out your own REVCANADA deduction and other source deductions.

BANK CHARGES

These are similar to a cavalry call.

Remember the trumpeter sounding the advance in the Cavalry with the officer in front screaming,

"CHARGE!!"

Well these are something like that.

As a prominent consultant once said, *"the details are whatever they are!"* This is not so with the banks. You are charged for every conceivable thing! Ever wonder why the banks are declaring such profits? Look at the following chart:

THIS IS ONE WAY THAT THE BANKS MAKE MONEY.

TYPES OF SERVICES	Royal	Scotia	CIBC	Montreal	TD	Avg		
Transaction								
Point of Sale	0.30	0.45	0.45	0.30	0.40	0.38	0.25	0.30
Memberlink								
Bill Payment	0.50	0.50	0.40	0.00	0.50	0.47	0.25	0.50
Monthly Flat Rate	2.95	2.95	0.00	3.00	0.00	2.96	0.00	0.00
Transfers	0.50	0.50	0.40	0.00	NIL	0.46	0.10	0.00
Inquiry Balance	0.50	0.50	0.45	0.00	NIL	0.48	0.10	0.00
Transaction List	0.50	0.50	0.00	0.00	1.00	0.66	0.00	0.00
PC Banking								
Bill Payment	3mo.free	n/a	$.45ea	0.00	$.60 ea	0.53	0.50	0.50
Monthly Flat Rate	$2.95/mo.	n/a	1st 20 free	13(MBANX)	n/a	7.97	0.00	0.00
Transfers	n/a	n/a	n/a	0.00	n/a	0.00	0.00	0.00
Inquiry Balance	n/a	n/a	n/a	0.00	n/a	0.00	0.00	0.00
ATM charge-other instit	1.25	1.00	1.00	1.00	free	1.06	1.00	1.00
International ATM charge	2.00	2.00	2.00	2.00	2.20	2.04	2.00	2.00
ATM transfer	0.50	0.50	0.50	0.50	0.40	0.48	0.00	0.00
Regular Cheque-Cheq clear	0.60	0.60	0.60	0.60	0.60	0.60	0.55	0.60
Monthly Statements-Personal	0.00	0.00	0.00	0.50	0.00	0.50	1.00	1.00
Statement Cheque Return	0.00	2.00	3.50	1.00	2.25	2.19	2.00	2.00
Package Account	9.50	9.95	9.50	8.85	12.00	9.96	9.50	9.50
Utility Bill Payment	1.25	1.30	1.50	1.25	1.35	1.33	1.25	1.30
Stop Payment	7.25	8.00	8.25	7.50	7.50	7.70	7.25	7.50
Preauthorized Debit	0.60	0.60	0.45	0.60	0.60	0.57	0.55	0.55
Business								
Charge Back	3.50	4.50	4.50	4.00	5.00	4.30	4.25	4.25
Cheque Clearing	0.60	0.60	0.60	0.60	0.60	0.60	0.70	0.70
Monthly Statements	0.00	0.00	6.00	4.50	3.75	4.75	4.50	4.50
RRSPs								
RRSP-Incoming	0.00	0.00	0.00	0.00	0.00	0.00	0.00	0.00
Saving RRSP Withdrawal Fee	0.00	0.00	0.00	25.00	0.00	5.00	0.00	25.00
RRSP transfer out	25.00	25.00	25.00	25.00	15.00	23.00	21.75	21.75
Drafts/Wires								
Draft-Canadian								
under $1000	3.25	3.25	3.25	3.25	6.75	3.95	5.00	4.00
over $1000	6.50	6.50	5.00	6.50	6.75	6.25	6.00	6.25
Drafts-US								
under $1000	6.25	6.25	4.50	3.25	3.25	4.70	5.00	4.00
over $1000	6.50	6.50	7.00	6.50	7.00	6.70	6.00	6.25

Have you ever had a conversation with your account executive regarding your bank charges? Do you even know who he or she is? You have to know as much as he or she knows. Be vigilant in your defense of not being charged unnecessary bank fees. Audit! That means go over everything. Find ways around being 'twenty-dollared' into submission. Remember you are the customer!

Yes, there is a charge for almost everything at a banking institution. Somewhere, somehow, someone figured out that they could charge for everything they did! The horror in the reality of small business is that most (read nearly all) small business people are too absorbed with the daily grind to realize all the charges that actually go on in banking. The spreadsheet below indicates the charges that are applicable for each action the businessperson requests.

Let's put another scenario on this. Let's visit Glenn Francis, the barber in our local barbershop.

- You walk in and there is a charge for that.
- You are seated in the chair and there is a charge for that.
- You are cloaked so there is a charge for that.
- The cloak is tied with a disposable piece of towel so there is a charge for that.
- Your hair is wetted. There is a charge for that.
- The barber cuts your hair, there is a huge charge for that (something like your monthly service charge).
- Then he uses the clippers, another charge.

- Then he soaps your neck with the warm smelly foam.
- Then he uses a straight razor - double charge.
- Don't forget the charge for trimming your beard, eyebrows, nose and other miscellaneous hairs.
- Powder and smelly stuff, you bet, another charge.
- Take the cloak off and brush off your clothes charge again!

Tell me now, who really wants to get their hair cut?

DISCOUNT RATE

This is another banking term.

This is the rate that the bank charges the merchant. Where's the discount? Who gets a discount? What discount are they talking about? Discount rate is the charge that the financial institution puts on every transaction that the merchant processes for people using their credit cards. Yes there is actually another service charge for the merchants accepting those indispensable cards:

- VISA
- MASTERCARD
- AMERICAN EXPRESS
- DINERS
- DEBIT CARD

That means that on every $100 sale the merchant loses 2% of the sale to the bank. The merchant is having their profit margin eroded AGAIN by the banks. Imagine the grief the merchant suffers when someone wants to pay for a two-dollar item with VISA. Well, you have to accept VISA, etc., as a merchant.

So that is why you are sometimes seeing minimum purchase requirement when using your credit card.

CREDIT CARD

The necessary plastic which is a part of our civilization.

These items are now indispensable parts of our culture. They are pieces of plastic that give the bearer the privilege of purchasing power. VISA used to be known as CHARGEX. Then along came MASTERCHARGE and the competition was launched.

Years ago, at the florist the tailor or the butcher, you could have your own personal charge account. Now you can charge anything everywhere. The credit card company takes a piece of the action. As a merchant you simply cannot operate without credit cards because everyone has them and uses them almost to the exclusion of cash.

The danger with credit cards is that they allow massive debt to be incurred by those people who hold the card. Debt has become a way of life for most people in our society. Debt *due* to credit card use.

Why don't the merchants say to customers:

> *"A BANK SERVICE CHARGE*
> *WILL BE LEVIED*
> *WHEN YOU USE YOUR*
> *CREDIT CARD."*

INDENTURED SLAVERY

Slang of the 90's and beyond.

This is the reality of retail. This is the reality of a franchise. This is the reality of being your own boss. Why slavery?

Because you are shackled to the immediacy of the moment.

In a franchise or any retail location you, as owner are not the master. You are the slave to all sorts of taskmasters. Who will buy your retail location when you have to sell? Will you get your investment back?

If you are an employee, you are also stuck. You cannot get out. Out means upgrading, which takes time and money. Generally, neither is available.

Indentured because there are all sorts of binding agreements surrounding the franchisee or the retailer. These assure the risk is solely on the side of the entrepreneur, and not that of the landlord, banker, or franchiser.

Because you are shackled to the immediacy of the moment.

LANDLORD

This is someone who owns the location in which your business currently resides.

The Landlord is an interesting phenomenon. The concept used to be of a kindly, elderly person renting to the young entrepreneurial idealist. The landlord was there to help the businessperson survive because, in turn, they helped the landlord by paying rent.

Today, things are somewhat different. Landlords can be anyone from who you thought was a friend to a holding company or a large corporate structure with layers upon layers of management. Today's landlords usually hold all the cards. There are interesting items like triple net which affect everything from your bottom line to cash flow. Landlords can either be roadblockers or flagpersons. The roadblockers put up barrier after barrier to block potential success. Flagperson-type landlords wave you on through. They promote their own properties, which in turn promote your business, which in turn increase your profits.

Be very careful when dealing with the landlord. Know their vocabulary. Understand what terms they offer. **Never sign a personal**

guarantee outside your company structure. A personal guarantee means that you are responsible not your limited company, not your DBA shell of a company. You and all that you have and hold personally are on the hook. This could include any personal commodity, which could mean your prize Labrador Retriever!

Have a lawyer read and <u>explain</u> whatever lease you have. Make sure you understand the lease. Remember the rent rule.

LANDLORD'S AGENT, MANAGEMENT COMPANY, SITE MANAGER

These are inventive nouns.

All these terms are synonymous. That means they sound different but have basically the same meaning. They possess both perceived power and real power. The larger leasing companies in Canada have a tiered structure in place to make it awkward for the lessee to be in actual contact with the lessor. It can also create some hilarious contrasts. For example, ask the same question of someone at each tier and you will often get a different answer from each person.

NEOPHYTES

This is a descriptor noun.

This is the descriptor noun used to portray people who are just starting out in small business. They often exhibit the following symptoms:

- unbridled enthusiasm;
- an unexplained air of euphoria;
- suffering from the "we can do it all and better syndrome."

This term only applies for three months or in some rare cases up to three years. Neophytes can cure themselves by hiring a small business consultant to help them leap correctly into the abyss of commerce.

Small Business Sucks

FEAR

This is a constant state of being.

Fear is **huge**.

It is an emotion that cloaks the day-to-day life of many small business people in Canada. Whenever there is a problem or situation, the very first reaction of the businessperson is fear. They suffer fear of the banks, fear of the landlord, fear of the tax man, fear of the competition, fear of the customer, fear of failure, fear of themselves.

The dictionary defines fear as an unpleasant emotion caused by **danger, pain, angst or worry**. It is obvious that the business climate causes the individual employer/owner constant fear.

A ripple effect can be seen in the behavior of the staff working in a workplace filled with uncertainty. The social implication is reflected again as this ripple effect extends itself into the families of those working for people in small business.

Fear is always waiting to burst out from behind the door of small business.

FUN

This is something of which we do not have enough.

Remember when we were young and we had real fun? Remember what we enjoyed having a lot? (That last sentence was a **solecism**, go ahead - look that one up, it will be fun.) In the morning, we had fun at recess and after school we had fun. *Fun is appreciation and mirth in day-to-day activities.* Re-invent fun in your day-to-day activities to release yourself from the mundane, the mediocre, and the morass that mires us through aging and routine.

PENCIL CASE

This is an essential small business tool.

Do you remember those pencil cases that the brown-nosers or the teacher's pet always carried with them? Well, what was really in them? Those kids who carried those pencil cases always got the awards at the end of the year. Mary Brown *pencil cased* her way through school and is now a CEO somewhere. You should now create your very own business pencil case. In your business pencil case you should place between five to ten dollars a day. At the end of the year, you would have a support fund between $1,825.00 and $3,650.00! This money can be used for any emergency. It can cover unexpected losses or become your cushion. Ten years of pencil casing could net between $18,250.00 and $30,650.00!!

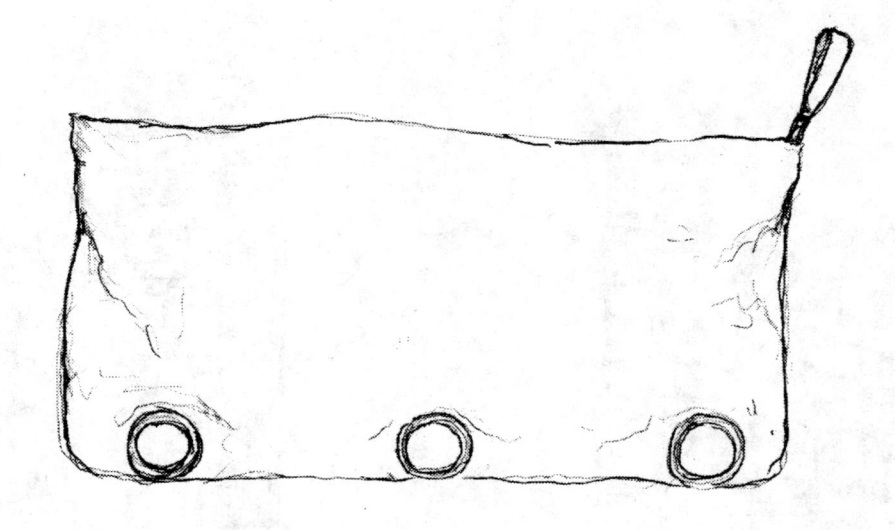

To order your own SBS Pencil Case, see contact info at back.

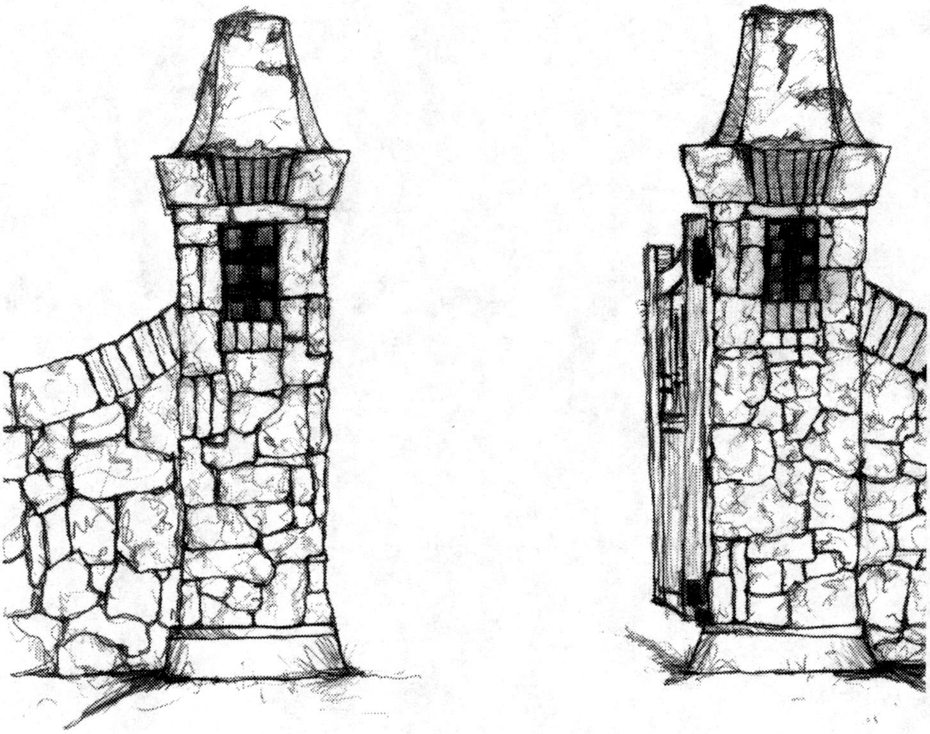

GATEKEEPERS

This is a term that is vital to success.

Gatekeepers are the receptionists, the secretaries, the maintenance persons, the mail carriers, the janitors, the delivery guys, the matrons and the security guards.

You know them. You look at them everyday.

See past their jobs. These are real people. It is these individuals who have the pulse of any given institution. They are the people who deny or give access.

Be civil. Treat them the way you want to be treated. Go out of your way to remember the names of their children and their spouse's name. Remember their birthday and know the names of their pets. You should also acknowledge them at Christmas or New Year's, or that special time of year that matches your niche's most important need. When you need access through their gate, it's a lot easier to have someone who will want to swing it open for you!

Small Business Sucks

HEADS UP

This is a business road sign.

This term comes from the vernacular or common language and should be seen by the person 'being given the heads up' as a red flag that says:

DANGER... ALERT... LOOK OUT... WATCH OUT... BE CAREFUL!

EMPLOYMENT INSURANCE COMMISSION
(Formerly known as UIC)

This is bureaucracy at its best.

This is a social safety net. It catches all Canadians who are temporarily out of work except small business owners. They are exempt. Yes! People are actually sitting in offices throughout Canada with a stamp to mark the forehead of any small business owner who becomes unemployed. Hundreds of their colleagues administer entitlement to billions of dollars when there is a staff member unemployed. There are lots of categories:

- maternity leave;
- paternity leave;
- sick leave;
- leave leave (I just made that one up;
- bereavement leave.

They also administer disability, immobility, inability, and capability. (There's not a lot of call for that last one.) All of this applies to everyone in Canada except ***small business owners.***

As an owner, don't ever object to one of your employees going on any one of these types of leaves. *Why???*

Because they'll call a tribunal. You know those things that they had lots of in ancient Rome. Once again, when you, as the employer objects to your contribution being spent in what you think is an inappropriate manner, you go up against the former employee who is now mad as a wet hen at you! You're holding up their claim! The tribunal is made up of retired UIC workers, or their aunts who have an opinion, and their lawyers. At this point all and sundry are advocates for the employee. Who is the advocate for the employer? You know the guy who is creating the jobs and paying the employer contribution! Who helps that business owner caught in the government bureaucracy?

The truth is out there - it's just impossible to find.

INSURANCE

This is a necessary evil.

Insurance is a fear-based commodity people must buy. All landlords require you to have the minimum amount of insurance to protect them in case of error on your part. It is a contract purchased to guarantee compensation for a specified loss by fire, death, etc.

Usually, acts of God are excluded. That of course means that when you really need the coverage, you don't have it.

Take the case of the Victoria restaurant owner, who when Victoria had 25 inches of snow during the Christmas of 1996 was shut out of his place of business. There weren't any snowplows in Victoria. He had his hydro and gas turned off as the landlord was afraid of fire. Consequently all his food for the New Year's Eve Party spoiled. He tried to claim on his insurance for the spoiled food and loss of business. Well, you guessed it. His insurance company said his loss wasn't covered. He could however have his lawyer file suit (read legal costs). He was told he had 60 days to file the suit after the adjuster's decision.

He chose not to sue. Yet, the money he was claiming would have helped his cash flow problems and given him some financial ease from the loss over one of his busiest times of the year.

SUICIDE

This is simply not an option.

The idea crosses the minds of more than one businessman and businesswoman. The idea of ending it all to ease the distress over bills and being pulled in a dozen different ways at once has been a mental playground for many. It is a sad state of affairs when taking one's own life for the eventual security of the life insurance policy is a possible out. To absent oneself from one's family and friends is simply NOT AN OPTION.

BEING IN ACTION

This is the antithesis of suicide.

Even though the roof may be falling in around you and even though you don't want to be in the particular predicament in which you are now, there are things you can do!

- Talk to someone, tell them about your troubles.
- Hire or contract a consultant.
- Create a support group. You would be surprised at how many people are in the same situation.
- Tell the truth. Tell the truth to yourself and others. How did you really end up in this current mess? Is this a repeating pattern in your life?
- Tell your family. Don't hide from them. They are the ones that love you.

Remember that old saying that when you need a friend, it is too late to make one? If you have to re-connect with a friend or mentor from your past, risk the truth with them.

"...risk the truth."

SUPPORT TEAM

This is an essential group.

The value of support cannot be under or over estimated. A support group can be as simple as one person or as complex as a formalized group of people. Their sole job is to support you in your vision, and its day-to-day creation. Whether things are rosy or falling apart, these people can form a bulwark for you in time of need and a cheering section when things go right.

PROFESSIONAL DEVELOPMENT

This is a term that involves personal growth.

- This is something we don't do enough of.
- This is something small business people do not normally do. There are a hundred reasons why we don't get around to listening to, hearing, or investigating other ways of doing things. Some of us become entrenched, develop myopia, or simply run out of funds. The beauty of developing ourselves is that it moves us from our comfort zone. It is something different.

Here are some professional development ideas:

Read any or all of the following:
- *The Wealthy Barber* by David Chilton;
- *Boom Bust and Echo* by David Foot;
- *Awaken the Giant Within* by Anthony Robbins.

Listen to the following tapes:
- *Meditations for People Who Do Too Much*;
- *Seven Things for Effective Management*, by Steven Covey;
- *The Celestine Prophecy*, by James Redfield.

Go to presentations sponsored by your local Chamber of Commerce, your merchant's association, the local college or university.

Do something different. Join a physical fitness class, take up Kendo, study the *I Ching Book of Change*.

Think outside the box. Try the following exercise:

Join the nine dots together using four straight lines. You cannot retrace a line or back track, nor can you lift your pen from the paper. Good Luck!

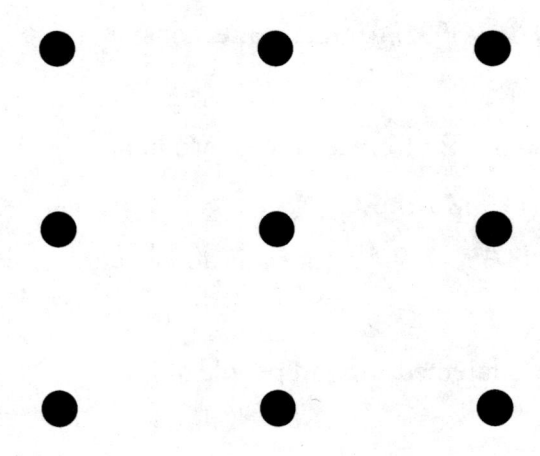

Create a support group or professional development group yourself. Align like-minded people to give each other feedback and support.

Here is a suggested list of professionals to help you:

- Hire a personal success coach.
   Michael Losier
   250-380-9282, mlosier@islandnet.com

- Play the Transformation Game.
   Mary Eshenko
   250- 382-6353

- Have your astrological chart cast.
   Georgia Nichols
   250-383-3005, georgia@direct.com

- Gain insight from a Psychic Medium.
   Carole Matthews
   1-888-350-9794, cmatth@islandnet.com

Call one of these talented support people today.

KINDNESS

A quality with consequences that few people really understand.

Kindness is quiet. It is unassuming. It is that act of extending yourself to your employees, your employer, your co-worker, your customers, or the person next to you. Kindness can be random. It also can be something, which you have thought about for a long time. Remember kindness is like friendship, once given it is always out there, always trying to work its way back to you.

INC., LTD.

These are legal terms.

According to the joint venture between the federal government and the provinces on small business the terms Ltd. or Inc. are the same. According to Ms. J. Bates, a lawyer from Calgary Alberta, the following is true. Under the Company's Act one can be incorporated and use any one of the following designations:

- Ltd. – Limited;
- Inc. – Incorporated;
- Co. - Company or their French equivalent.

MINISTRY OF LABOUR
This is a euphemism for a collection of people in authority who are bumblers.

Each province in Canada has this collection of people who minister to the workers who are employed in every sector of our society. It tells the owners of small business what they can and cannot do. They have sweeping powers. They are populated by autocratic bureaucrats. They are advocates for anyone but the employer. They never listen to the side of the employer. The employer is presumed guilty the instant a former worker complains.

Ministries of Labour are populated with mid- level bureaucrats who do not work in, or understand the real world. They postulate ridiculous, unworkable, and unenforceable rules for the small business owner. They dictate overtime rules, and sanction the worker's holiday rights (there are no holiday rights for employers) known as statutory holidays. That's right! There are days during the year when the owner of the business actually has to pay their staff and give them the day off. Whoever thought that up?

Additionally, if an employee works on a statutory holiday they are awarded time and one half for wages. *Why?* Are they working harder? That is *why* you see the owners working on those statutory holidays. Pity the restaurant owner who has to staff for things like Christmas and New Year's. Their costs go up proportionally.

Most small business owners are not that familiar with the dictates of these **ministries of truth.** There is actually an ordinance in one of these empires that states if an employee is required to wear protective clothing for the job then the employer is to have them dry cleaned, clean them himself, or award the employee $2.68 per week for cleaning whatever it is the employee wears. To find out more, call the numbers listed on the next page for each province.

* The thesaurus gives the following synonyms for the word euphemistic: insincere, suave, affected, pretentious, theatrical, and mealy mouthed.

Alberta 403-427-8541

British Columbia 604-660-4000

Manitoba 204-945-3352

Newfoundland 709-727-2743

New Brunswick 506-453-3902

Nova Scotia 902-424-4311

Ontario 416-326-7004

Prince Edward Island 902-892-3416

Quebec 514- 873-7076

Saskatchewan 306-787-2438

CAPITAL

This is something you need.

No it is not like Toronto, Ottawa, Washington or Paris. It is, however, something you need.

It is "*money, money, money, money, money,...*" (sung to the tune from that great hit show, *Cabaret*).

You need lots of it.

When you think you have enough, trust me, you are under capitalized. Seriously, capital is the term applied to the value of the investment made by a person in any business or undertaking.

CAPITAL EXPENDITURE

This is usually a lot of money.

This is money spent to acquire or improve buildings and equipment. This usually means your money. However this can be injected money. You can add new shareholders. These are people with additional money to add to the company's share base. It can also be partnered by a financial institution but they usually want secured assets (like your house) or a Guaranteed Security Agreement, commonly know as GSA, against the leasehold improvement.

CAPITAL GAIN

This is usually a myth.

This is the profit made on the sale of an asset. Your lawyer, your accountant, and Revenue Canada all have different definitions as to what this actually means.

GSA

This is another secret code.

This is a term banks and lending institutions throw around the same way that a florist will speak Latin. *"Would you like some gypsophilia with your agapanthus?"* Couldn't they just say, *"do you want baby's breath with your lily?"* A sheet salesman will speak thread counts per square inch or tcpsi. Like everybody knows that!!!

It's the secret vocabulary that the person on the outside of everything needs to acquire.

The initials mean **Guaranteed Security Agreement**.

This is something each bank takes on the individual's inventory or their equipment, or in some cases their leasehold improvements.

BALANCE SHEET

This is a term for all small business people.

Well, you saw this coming. No, it is not a sheet trying to balance itself, nor is it a teeter-totter wrapped in your linen. It is, however, a financial statement showing a detailed list of the assets, liabilities, and capital of a business on a certain date.

N

NSF CHARGES

This is another banking term.

So if there isn't sufficient money for the cheque to clear in the first place, how can there possibly be a charge for Non-Sufficient Funds??

ADVERTISING

This item is fun, but costly.

This is something that is truly worthwhile in the daily grind of the business world. However, it is expensive.

Advertising really works! Consider this quiz:

- What is "finger lickin'" good?
- What is the "real thing?"
- What airline company was the "wings of man?"
- Where do you "deserve a break today?"
- Who is the "great American hero?"
- Who "gets rid of grease and grime in just a minute?"

The answers are:

- Kentucky Fried Chicken;
- Coke;
- Eastern Airlines;
- Macdonald's ;
- G.I. Joe;
- Mr. Clean.

If you answered this in quick time then you have just confirmed the fact that advertising works.

Point of Interest

If you repeat something twenty-one times it becomes a subconscious fact. If your target market is bombarded with a name, or a phone number, or a moniker then you have a customer for life.

The exercise here is to create some logo that will put your company in the same league as those above. It is necessary to imbed your name in the consciousness of the consumer. The buying public must be able to make that link between thought and purchase.

Some examples of this are:

- Thornhill's Florist...implying that there is only one that qualifies to meet the need of this upscale neighbourhood.
- *"phone PIZZAPIZZA, 967-1111"*
- This phone number = PIZZA. The subliminal message here is PHONE US AND YOU GET PIZZA!
- *"The Smile is in the aisle for you."* Thrifty Foods
- Moore's *The Suit People* (like no one else sells suits????)

Now take the name of your business and create.

_____ _____

_____ _____

_____ _____

_____ _____

_____ _____

MONIKER

This is an advertising term.

This is a term that has some punch!

It is a nickname that creates a consciousness of your company and your product by just saying it. Here's an exercise for this term.

Take into consideration regional disparities. Then make your company indispensable to that area. For example, when you think of:

- ketchup ....you think of *HEINZ*
- mustard..you think of *FRENCH'S*
- coffee..you think of *JUAN VALDEZ*

Now make it work for yourself:

_____   _____

_____   _____

STAFF MEETINGS

This is usually the forum for the boss's opinions.

Staff meetings are an occasion when we assert that we are all in the same boat.

Staff meetings are important. The following is an easy, no fuss, step-by- step schedule or format for your meetings.

AGENDA

- Social: coffee, tea and the Boss's Bundt Cake (recipe to follow)

- Good morning/afternoon and **welcome!** Identify the time/quarter of the year you are in and the upcoming events like Christmas.

- Get to the heart of the meeting like staffing, new procedures, money issues, protocols, etc.

- Try to have staff present for part of the meeting. Acknowledge some staff for their accomplishments. Have a 'Golden Foot' award for the staff member who has recently put his or her foot in their mouth. Make sure, that the boss gets the award at least once a year. Finish up with old business from the last meeting and new business. Call for agenda items for next meeting.

- Smile. It's infectious!

Staff meetings allow a monthly focus. They get all the staff together. (This is a drawback in some provinces where casual help must be paid a minimum of four hours if they show up for a scheduled staff meeting which may only last twenty minutes. The individual could agree to come in at no remuneration.)

Staff meetings can be useful as information distribution. Remember, everyone hears things differently. It is a good idea to always have a written component to the verbal presentation.

Sometimes it feels like the bosses are in his/her own boat all by themselves. Staff meetings help to get everyone in the same boat rowing the same way at peak times. Staff meetings can be instructive when presenting new routines or skills to be incorporated in the day-to-day fabric of the routine.

The Boss's Bundt Cake

1 2/3 cups of all-purpose flour

1 1/2 cups of white or brown sugar

1/2 cup of cocoa

1 1/2 teaspoons of baking soda

1 teaspoon of salt

1/2 teaspoon of baking powder

2 eggs

1/2 cup of shortening

1 1/2 cups of buttermilk or sour milk

1 teaspoon of vanilla extract

Heat oven to 350 degrees.

Generously grease and flour a 12-cup bundt pan. In a large mixer bowl blend flour, sugar, cocoa, baking soda, salt, and baking powder.

Add remaining ingredients and beat or blend on low speed for one minute. Scrape the mixture from the sides of the bowl. Beat on high speed for three minutes, scraping the mixture occasionally.

Pour the mixture into prepared bundt pan.

Bake 50 to 55 minutes at 350 degrees. Cool 10 minutes (really 1/2 hour).

Then turn cake out onto wire rack or serving plate.

Make it look great by dusting with white icing sugar and shaved light and dark **Dutch** chocolate.

Do this the night before. You won't have time to fuss the morning of the staff meeting!!!!

GAME FACE

This is a psychological tool.

This is something every small businessperson must have. You are either in the game or out of the game. To be in the game you must be perceived to be playing. This means that your personal problems, your cash flow, your supplier problems, your sales projections, your landlord problems and your tax arrears, are all hidden carefully behind the game face. The game face tells your employees, your suppliers and most importantly, the buying public that we're open for business and we will do the very best we can for you. Here are some comments that could revolve around the GAME FACE:

"Is my game face in place this morning?"

"Let me know if my game face slips would you?"

"Great game face today!"

"Would you mind if I took my game face off and had a conversation with you?"

Small Business Sucks

Small Business Sucks

88

KARMA

This is a spiritual mirror.

Karma is the quality or a force generated by a person's actions. It will affect what happens in this and the next life. It is a tenet of those who practice the religions of Hinduism and Buddhism. Some of us have better karma than others.

KARMA

卡玛

因缘

Q

QUARTERS

This is business vocabulary.

No, these are not the Mountie quarters. These are like fractions for the year. There are four quarters in a year. Each quarter has three months. The language skill for this term is: *"In the first quarter we were sluggish due to intemperate conditions out of the U.S. However, we recouped in the second and third quarter (sounds vaguely like football) and shot through the roof in the fourth quarter due to strong year end demands"* (they mean Christmas).

ATTITUDE

This quality is a lifesaver!

It is more important than the past,

than education,

than money,

than circumstances,

than success,

than what other people think or say or do.

It is more than appearance, giftedness, or skill.

It will make or break a company, a church, a home.

The remarkable thing is we have a choice every day regarding the attitude we will embrace for that day.

We cannot change our past... we cannot change the fact that people will act in a certain way.

We cannot change the inevitable.

The only thing we can do is play on the one string we have, and that is our attitude...

The longer I live, the more I realize the impact of attitude on life.

Attitude is more important than facts.

I am convinced that life is 10% what happens to me and 90% how I react to it.

And so it is with you...

We are in charge of our attitudes.

COMMITMENT

This is a quality rarely found.

This term is for every segment of society.

Be careful what commitments you make.
They often become engagements that restrict your freedom.
Commitment is something that you can't break.
Commitment is something that keeps you hidebound to the task.
Commitment becomes an obligation.
Commitment can shackle as surely as any pair of handcuffs.
Commitment once kept can give a great sense of accomplishment and then you'll know that...

Commitment is what transforms a promise into reality. It is the words that speak boldly of your intentions, and the actions that speak louder than the words. It is making the time when there is none. Coming through time after time, year after year. Commitment is the stuff character is made of, the power to change the face of things. It is the daily triumph of integrity over skepticism.

Commitment

Until one is committed, there is hesitancy, the chance to draw back, always ineffectiveness concerning all acts of initiative and creation. There is ONE elementary truth, the ignorance of which kills countless ideas and splendid plans: that the moment one definitely commits oneself, then Providence moves too. All things occur to help one that would never otherwise have occurred. A whole stream of events issue from the one decision, raising in one's favour all manner of unforeseen incidents and material assistance which no man could have dreamed would have come his way.

Whatever you can do or dream, you can. Begin it.

Boldness has genius, power, and magic in it. *Begin it now.*

...BY GOETHE

FAITH

A quality all small business people must have.

It is belief without evidence.

INTEGRITY

Another quality rarely found.

Integrity is something that has boundaries. It is a quality that many people are hard pressed to describe accurately.

- The 'real' dictionary defines integrity as honesty, the quality of telling the truth.
- It is NOT just the truth when its convenient, or okay, or when the truth puts the speaker in the right light. It is the truth. Not the honest truth or the real truth.
- Simply the truth.
- What would the truth look like if one of your customers asked you if you were gouging? What would the truth look like if someone asked you if your prices were fair?
- It is the truth all the time. No white lie or exaggeration lies allowed.

That is difficult. Have you ever tried it? Try just for one day to tell the truth in every single aspect of your day. No matter what.

Tell the truth to the first people you meet in the morning and the last person you see in the evening and for the encore tell the truth all over again the next day! Hopefully it will become a habit.

TRUST

This too, is a much-needed quality.

This is the assured reliance on the character, ability, strength, or truth of someone or something. It is the belief and hope that events will unfold in the manner in which they are meant to be.

COMMUNICATION

This is a necessary quality.

This is the ability to impart information, to share, to get your point across. This is a lot more complex than it sounds. The traditional communicator does so in the Socratic method. That is, I speak - you listen.

There are those in the business world who, if *they* want your opinion, *they* will give it to *you*.

The reality in today's world is that employees, and all people that surround the small businessperson, have been empowered. Sometimes this has happened for good reason. They deal on a day-to-day basis with the customers, the phones, the suppliers and they impart information. They also represent you and your company.

They can either all be a bunch of loose cannons or they can be trained. Now, is the small businessperson an expert in his chosen field or a communicator? There is great value in hiring a communications consultant. The area of expertise is taken away from the owner and filled by a third party. Then everyone learns the same communication model. *"Presto, chango!"* The dynamics of the workplace are changed forever! Why? Because everyone is communicating more effectively.

It's bottom line better sharing. Also it makes a better bottom line.

END OF THE DAY ROUTINE

This is a term to make habits sound not so monotonous.

The value in having an end of the day routine is that things get accomplished with some regularity and uniformity.

For example, when the work day is done:

- take your cash register reading;
- distribute your money;
- have a float for the next day ready;
- do your cleanup;
- check the lights and the heat;
- set the alarm;
- lock the door;
- skip to your car!

START OF THE DAY ROUTINE

See above and reverse it!!

TREND

A repetitive item.

Actually the synonym for this word is fad. You remember fads like the pet rock, the lava lamp, the hooded sweatshirt, and the 'Nehru' jacket? With fads, it is imperative to know when to get in and when to get out. There are still some overly enthusiastic buyers who have boxes of Nehru jackets sitting in the warehouses of those big name clothing stores waiting for the 'Memories of the Millennium' sale that will occur on Dec. 26, Boxing Day, 2000! That, of course, will be a statutory holiday in Canada.

RELLI

This is an employee secret code.

This is a term used by employees. It is descriptive in nature. It refers to the sons, daughters, cousins, nieces, nephews, aunts or uncles, or in-laws, of the employer. Some of them are dreaded because they could easily be coming to a workstation near them. Remember they are those who can do no wrong! Read the relative section, entitled 'A Slice of Life.'

Send us your own stories of the relatives where you work. Let us know who gets hired, who gets fired! How does being a relative of the boss affect what really goes on at work?

LINEUPEE

This is something of which you've been a part.

A member of a line. A person standing in line at a National Coffee Store or the local equivalent waiting for a tall double foamy wet wet latte with chocolate sprinkles on top. Alternatively, a person waiting to check out anywhere at the local Quickie Mart, a convenience store or waiting endlessly for a teller at your local credit union or chartered bank branch.

Point of Interest

Lineupees are known for spontaneous conversation with one another.

These are all potential LINEUPEES

SHARES/ASSETS

This is a legal term.

Okay, this is a good one!

Shares exist in a registered company. That is a company now called LTD., the English term, LTEE., the French term, or INC., which is the American term. The company has two distinct parts. They are the shares of the company and the assets.

For most small businesses the shares belong to the directors of the company. The assets belong to the intrinsic domain of the company. Some of the assets that companies have are their lease, leasehold improvements, stock and inventory (may include vehicles) and bank loans. The assets of a company may be sold.

There are private companies and public companies. Private companies have less than fifty shareholders and form about 90% of the companies in Canada. The rest are public companies and their shareholders are not directors.

SHAREHOLDER'S LOAN

This is a company benefit.

This is a method by which the directors of the company can be repaid. First, of course, they must have lent, injected or otherwise infused the money into the corporation. For example a small retail company needs to purchase inventory. There is $10,000.00 in one of the director's personal bank accounts. The director loans the company that money to purchase the stuff (inventory) to sell. Theoretically when the inventory is sold the director is repaid his or her loan.

DIRECTOR

This is a legal descriptor.

Under the Companies Act for each province there must be directors of a registered company. That's right - someone who is *responsible* for the actions of the company. They are usually a president and a secretary/treasurer who are registered at the corporate headquarters.

You **can** get by with only one person registering as a director. To date in each province that person must be a resident of that province.

RESPONSIBILITIES

These are things the small businessperson has.

There are certain protective elements in being a small registered company in Canada. However, being a registered company incurs some responsibilities. Here are some of the most important:

- You must hold an Annual Meeting of Directors. That meeting must result in the filing of your annual report to the Ministry of Finance. They issue a form two weeks before the anniversary of incorporation. This form is sent to the company's agent (usually your lawyer); for an added fee it can go to another address. You bet there is an annual fee for filing. Currently, it is $35.00 in B.C. The penalty for not filing is that your company can be struck from the Registrar's list. Consequently, your company will cease to exist. You have three years and two months grace period for filing. Of course, you must pay for each year's filing.

- You must report your annual earnings (year-end) and file and pay federal taxes.

- You must report and pay GST. Currently there is director's liability for this. That means if your company is unable to pay then the director must pay any and all arrears.

- You must report, submit and pay the employer portion for source deduction for Revenue Canada.

- You must follow the LABOUR code for each province re: standards and practices for employers.

SALES REP

Think of an aisle of soup cans. Each flavour could be a different salesman.

You know, we are all acquainted with these ladies and gentlemen of commerce. They are the ones with the pulse on whatever industry. They know all the gossip, and usually spread it around like peanut butter. They come in with a big smile, know the staff, and want only one thing- your money (see profit margin).

These people are not to be confused with gatekeepers. Their agenda is to do only one thing and that is sell, sell, sell, sell! Often, they will try to get you to agree to terms (see terms).

PROFIT MARGIN

This is a fiction-filled idiom.

This is the **percentage** that belongs to you after everything else is paid. All the money you have left after your gross dollar volume for the month belongs to you.

The equation looks like this:

- you pay the rent;
- you pay the bank loan;
- you pay the phone bill and the yellow pages ad which is usually built into the cost of the phone bill,;
- you pay for the Internet access;
- you pay for the hydro/electricity;
- you pay for the gas for the company vehicle;
- you pay for your inventory;
- you pay for the coffee supplies for the staff;

- you pay the staff;
- you pay the employer deductions, which include employer contributions;
- you pay the 7% of each sale that you have collected for the Government of Canada;
- you pay the percentage you collected for the provincial government;
- you pay yourself;
- what is left over can be calculated as your profit . It is something % of your gross sales, or of the total money you have brought in that month!

TERMS

These can be the cement shoes for many small businesses.

These are something wholesalers give their purchasers. Also, this is something that unsuspecting neophytes take.

Do not make that mistake because:

- At the bottom of most invoices is a trite little comment that says something like, 'net 15 days.' That means you must pay this bill in **15 days.**

- Overdue accounts charged 2% per month - **that is 26.8% annually!**

- All expenses incurred in collecting past due accounts will be charged to the purchaser. **This means if you get behind in payments, you will have to pay all the expenses incurred in their collection process, including collection agents fees, court costs, bailiff costs, photocopy costs, etc.**

While you may like the latitude or the seeming latitude of terms, you don't want to position your supplier to be able to beat you up with their terms should things turn sour. Instead say, " yes, I'll agree to terms, my terms" and cross out the 2%, and other things you find not to be workable. If they agree to your terms, then go ahead.

UNDER THE TABLE

This is generally an employee's request.

From time to time the employer will be asked *"Will you just pay me quietly under the table."* The request behind the question is that the employee is paid their wages without taxes, and other deductions being reported. The danger behind this request is that there is no write off for the employer. The greater danger here is that the employee in a tiff goes to the Labour Board, a division of the Ministry of Labour, and then makes a federal case of the employer doing what he/she was asked to do in the first place.

The caution here for this term is:

Don't use the table for anything other than putting things on or eating.

RECONCILIATION

This is a term of the last century.

This is not a reunion between parents and children. It is not the sacrament of penance in the Roman Catholic Church. It is, however, the process of bringing into agreement the balance as shown by the bank statement and the balance shown by your cash book.

STATEMENT OF ACCOUNT

This used to be a monthly occurrence.

This is a detailed statement of a customer's account showing debits, credits, and unpaid balance. This is usually prepared monthly. This is also a job that a gatekeeper usually guards with his or her life. There should be clear cut boundaries regarding the following:

- Is there a monthly re-billing charge?
- Is the company entitled and allowed by law to charge interest?
- Has the customer agreed to pay either the re-billing charge or the interest charge?
- Does your statement indicate that payment is due upon receipt of the statement?

- Are there monthly statement stuffers to entice the customer to buy again??
- How does your company deal with unpaid accounts? Is it stated somewhere on the bill or statement you issue or that the customer has signed?
- Do both the customers and the staff know the person who can solve problems with customer accounts? Is there more than one person with that knowledge?
- Do you know why you **ALLOW** charge accounts?
- How is the account aged? Aging is the point at which interest or re-billing charges are added.
- As you are reading these statements, do you know what they mean?

DEBIT CARD

This is a bank toy.

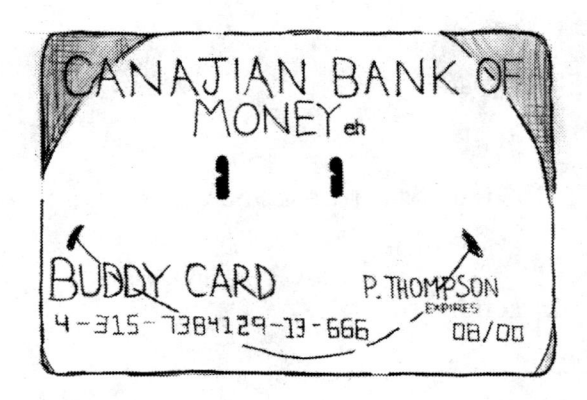

Do you think we are moving to a cashless society? It certainly will be if we keep this up.

Debit Cards are an instant access to your money. That is what the banks tell you but is it really the truth?

Example

Let us pretend that we are going to the grocery store and you use your Debit card on a $10.00 purchase. To use POS (point of sale) for example on a $10.00 purchase in the grocery store or for gas at the gas station it costs the consumer between 20 and 30 cents *per purchase*.

So, in the world of spreadsheets, that means, if you use your debit card ten times per week you would pay:

- $2.00 per week
- $10.00 per month
- $120.00 per year

If you use the POS 20 times per week you would pay: $4.00 per week

- $6.00 per month
- $208.00 per year.

There are some accounts that are exempt.

Point of Interest

If there are 10,000 debit cards being used 20 times a week, the bank receives $40,000.00 in revenue from user fees.

Now that's worthy of note by itself. The really fascinating part of this whole scenario is that every time the merchant accepts a debit card, they pay as well. They are being charged for a service they are providing. The bank is charging as little as fifteen cents per transaction. This is seemingly a small fraction of a $100.00 sale. What kind of miser would balk at such a puny fee? After all, fifteen cents is a measly fraction of a $100.00 sale. You must remember, however, that it is fifteen cents for every sale. Now let's look at this from the bank's perspective. After all is there *any other* perspective?

The merchant logs eighty sales per eight-hour period at fifteen cents per sale or $12.00 daily.

This amounts to $4,380.00 per year.

Point of Interest

Ten thousand debit cards being used twenty times a week equals $30,000.00 per week from the retail side.

The purchasers pay:	$40,000.00/week to the bank
The merchants pay:	$3,000.00/week to the bank
The purchasers pay:	$480,000.00/quarter to the bank
The merchants pay:	$36,000.00/quarter to the bank
The purchasers pay:	$2,080,000.00/year to the bank
The merchants pay:	$156,000.00/year to the bank

Please realize that this sample is only based on 10,000 cards being used a mere 20 times a week. Think of the seasonal adjustments like Christmas, Easter, Mother's Day, and summer/winter vacation.

One retailer who owns a 24 hour gas bar and food store had to pay the bank $3,586.00 during the month of September in 1997.

Now, let's see – if, in Canada, there were:

> 10,000 24-hour gas bars X an average of $3,500.00 =
> would you believe $35,000,000.00?
> $35,000,000.00 X 12 = $420,000,000.00

I guess it is relatively easy to see why the banks are encouraging the use of debit cards.

The bank also charges the merchant a yearly or monthly rental for that point of sale terminal. The merchant needs a separate or dedicated phone line because we all know that customers just love to use that secret code on their card.

Debit Cards can look like this:

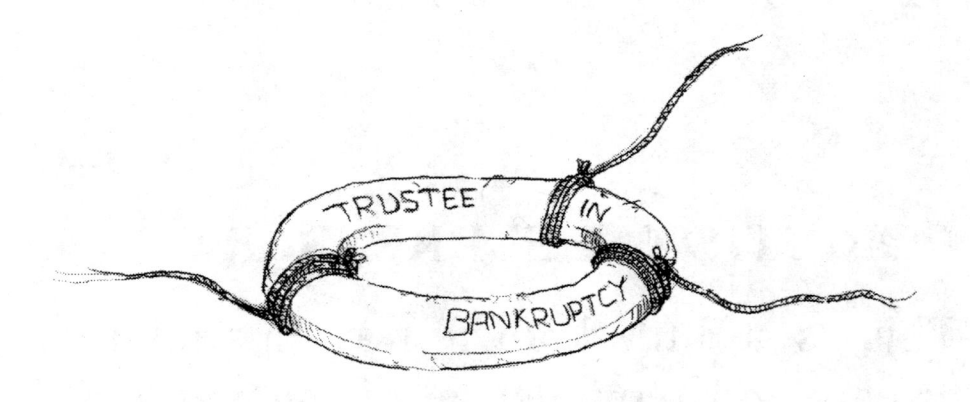

TRUSTEE IN BANKRUPTCY

This is a person who specializes in bankruptcy and insolvency.

This person is often a lifesaver for many.

This is a person or corporation to whom you have entrusted or given over your business affairs. These people know the ropes. They are smart, unique and have original solutions to age-old problems.

Trust them and be unfailingly honest with them.

CONDITIONAL SURRENDER

This is a little-known way around rent arrears and reminds me of *unconditional* surrender.

When you are in rent arrears, this is something that the landlord may ask you to do. **Don't.**

It means that you voluntarily give the lease back to the landlord. With this approach, you don't have any rights or protection. The landlord can throw you out at his or her pleasure and the landlord can assign the lease to whomever they choose, and you still owe the arrears.

PETTY CASH

This is a myth.

That's a good one. Petty cash may exist in large corporations, governments, schools, churches and layered organizations. It is supposed to be used for non-capital items and things that are of a consumable nature. Usually petty cash is found in a gray metal box with a key that a gatekeeper guards with his or her life. In small business, petty cash is most often in the pocket or the purse of the boss.

PETTY CASH BOX

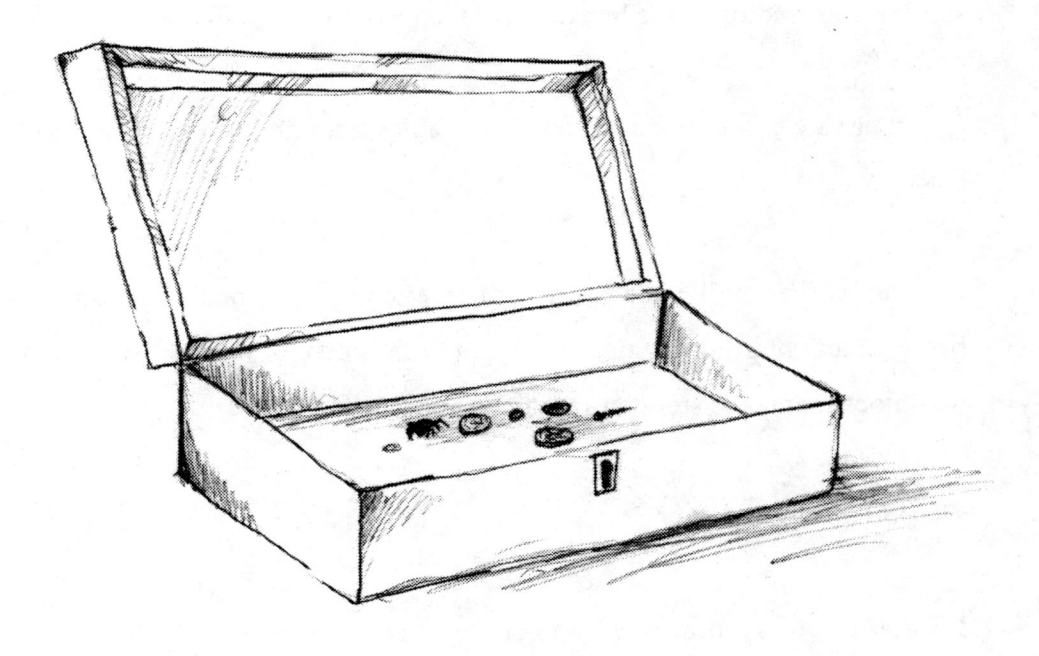

GUTS

This is vernacular.

This is a term that could easily be a quality (see the section on quality, generally but not always found under the letter Q).

Guts are the intestinal fortitude that allows the small business owner to wear his or her game face. It is the quality that enables the business owner to put the key in the door and wrestle the suppliers, the civil service, the landlords, the bankers and then of course, the public.

It is that rare piece of inner self that enables and empowers you on a daily basis.

Guts allow the small business owner to try and make it, on a day-to-day basis, in an environment that is fraught with potential failure, constant roadblocks, and a system unfriendly to success.

The advice here is:

It takes a fair amount of guts to run a small business.

BANK COMMUNICATION

This is something banks don't do.

Unless there is something negative to tell you, banks generally don't talk to you.

Reproduced with permission.

VOICE MAIL

This new age service is possibly the most annoying roadblock in the communication sector today.

"Hi, you've reached Joe Spledunk and I am not here to take your call at the moment. If you would like to leave a message, press three, if you would like the company directory press four and enter the first seventeen digits of the name of the person you are trying to reach; please note there is no allowance for the letter 'Q'." (Why is the person I'm always trying to reach named Alan Quartermain?). How many of us would like to tell these people they can press something else?

Or how about this one:

"Hi, this is Bank Savage and it is Friday the 24th. I am in the office all day and at meetings (actually I am hiding in the coffee room trying to avoid doing any work at all and then blaming lack of productivity on some underling). If you need immediate assistance, forget it, the whole floor is in here with me."

Here are two realities:

1. Voice mail allows people to hide from their work as the following story illustrates:

   I actually called a local bank located in the same mall as my business. I could see them in the window all having a hilarious time. I kept the line open, went over to the bank and walked right into the room. *"Is there no-one on the phones today - I need a few questions answered. All of you are in the same room and no one is helping customers. What are you really being paid for?"* I inquired self- righteously.

2. The creator of voice mail was a genius; but voice mail has taken on the following qualities:

- It can be a huge disservice to people.
- It can be a pain in the ass and a roadblock to success.
- It can be a cloak for people who have all sorts of personal agendas that they bring to work.
- It can and does deny access to people who need it the most.
- It can prevent the little guy from getting the information.

Whether there are questions or answers that need to be dealt with, voice mail can block them all.

WHOLESALE/RETAIL

These are terms that no longer mean what they once did.

The western marketing system is based on the wholesale/retail model. This is basically a two-tier system. The retailer is the person who markets the merchandise throughout their stores, storefronts, stalls, or whatever.

They own the U-brew, the garden specialty store, the trendy stationery store, the hairdressing salon, the florist, the bakery, the shoe store, the chocolate store and the book store.

All of these people buy their merchandise from the wholesaler, jobber, and other suppliers. The wholesaler collects, corrals, and coerces their products from the manufacturers, the growers, and the middlemen. They are the co-operative that acts as distribution or clearing houses to the retailers who supply to the public. *Right??* Wrong!!

Not right anymore!!

Today there is little or no clear-cut distinction between the wholesaler and the retailer.

So, once again who is caught in the middle??

WRITE OFF

This is shrouded in business myths and mists.

Well, sometimes a myth. A business guru once said you can't write off anything unless you have the money to do it. Sage advice.

For example, you cannot get tax money back unless you have paid it in the first place. Another method is to claim against taxes paid in prior years. *However*, if you are diligent you can write off lots. A write off is a purchase you make that will be absorbed by the company. To know what write offs you can use, you can either read the Income Tax Act, which changes constantly. Or you could rely on the ability of paid tax professionals including your accountant. Aren't they small business people with the same problems as you??

Samples of write offs:

- Gas for business travel;
- Cellular phone costs;
- Breakfasts, lunches, dinners as long as you are knoshing with a client;
- Dog food for your guard dog (including guard poodles);
- Work boots if you are in construction;
- Coffee for the staff;
- Let us know your most unusual write off!

MARK UP

This is something that small business retailers do to their prices.

Small business people use this term to refer to the cost over purchase price. To those not in retail, its the all inclusive total on an individual piece of merchandise. This is the way the retailer recoups his/her outlay and creates their profit margin. Sounds confusing? It is! No two retailer/small business persons can or will give you the same answer. A Christmas tree costs the retailer $1.00 the purchaser pays $2.50. The mark up is 2.5.

For example:

- The local grocery store operates on a much smaller margin than a specialty store. They can, in fact, buy cases and cases of soup and sell it for pennies less than cost... because it will bring in the hordes to buy the meat, or in-store bakery or produce on which they are making a killing.

Generally the retailer will mark things up double or more from the price they purchase from the supplier. If it costs one hundred dollars your specialty shop will sell it for two hundred dollars.

BOOK VALUE

This is yet another legal and accounting term.

No, it is not how much your personal collection of books is worth. It is the value ascribed to your company assets by applying a formula for depreciation over time against the date and purchase price of your equipment, inventory, leasehold improvements and enhancements.

Book value is the cost of a fixed asset less its accumulated depreciation. For example, your $1500.00 cash register is written off by $300.00 depreciation each year. It takes five years to write down to nothing.

WIZ

The short form for wizard.

This is what they call a really good boss or employer. A Wiz, just like his namesake the Wizard of Oz, can and often does perform miracles.

X

XENOGASAPHOBIA

This is a word like supercalafragalisticexpialadoscious.

If anyone reading this knows the meaning of this word please email its meaning to us.

VARIABLE

This is the '*x*' in any equation.

The circumstances surrounding our day-to-day routines are to some degree changeable. These can be due to the weather, our health, our karma or the course our relationships take. These are the variables that make up our lives. They can be altered to some extent by how we plan.

Variables include things like the weather, your marriage or relationship, who has just died, or given birth, your car, how your sports team is doing, how well your son or daughter is or is not doing in school or life in general, your weight, your hair, your pets, your suppliers, and your horoscope.

PLAN

This is an invaluable tool.

It has often been said that people don't plan to fail but that they do fail to plan.

Time and time again, I have asked people if they have taken a vacation. The answer is invariably, *"yes."* The next question is usually met with some positive affirmation. When I ask them how long they took to plan their holiday, they go into hordes of detail as to how they planned their vacation and how much time the planning took.

When I ask how much time have they spent in planning their business or their life this blank look usually comes over them. People simply fail to plan their lives which includes their businesses or professions as well.

The following is a visual to plan eighteen months ahead. One client told me she had never planned eighteen minutes ahead let alone eighteen months.

Having completed this exercise her life not only looks a lot different but is a lot different!

On this piece of paper - yes, right here in this book, write down the top four goals you have for your business or your life.

- _____

- _____

- _____

- _____

Now, on this page write how you are going to accomplish the four goals from the previous page.

They can be one-word action descriptors, or whole sentences.

- _____

- _____

- _____

- _____

On the next two pages plan the next eighteen months of your life. Include such life milestones as birthdays, anniversaries, and your business life. Seasonal highs and lows should be marked in a different colour. Use the next two pages as a map, or blueprint, or strategy for your personal and professional future.

From this you can make it happen, instead of letting it happen to you!

1._____

2._____

3._____

4._____

5._____

6._____

7._____

8._____

9._____

10._____

11._____

12._____

13._____

14._____

15._____

16._____

17._____

18._____

YURT

This was the original sales cart. It was the forerunner to the barrow full of flowers, the gypsy wagon, the lunch truck, the hot dog cart, the cart full of stuff, and just about every other sales gimmick on wheels.

CANADA/USA COMPARISON

Canada is next to the United States of America. The business and bank contrasts are enormous!

In the United States of America there are roughly 3,500 banks and financial institutions to service a population of some 267 million people or roughly one bank for every six million people. In Canada there are five banks soon to be two or three and several credit unions to service a population of some thirty million people. This is soon to be one bank for approximately eight million people.

The contrasts in Canadian/American banking laws will be examined in our soon-to-be-released American edition.

Point of Interest

Some of the banks say that they are interested in servicing small businesses. All of the banks tie the loan requirements to the personal financial profile of the small business owner. As many of us know, mechanics drive cars in need of repair, and the shoemaker's family needs shoes. Well, the business owner's finances are usually terrible. The banks, in most cases, will not assume the risk of business loans.

BOUNDARIES

These are imaginary lines that keep countries from flowingintooneanother.

Boundaries also show where you can and cannot go. These are important lines for the employer to know. It is also important for all to know when and how to draw these lines. They establish clear-cut definitions. For example: *"this is what I will do as the boss and this is what I expect you to do as the employee."*

In the real world though, boundaries become fluid. The employer can be easily manipulated. He becomes the indentured service person to the employees. The value in establishing a set of boundaries is one of consistency. Additionally, boundaries help keep routines in place. Establishing boundaries and procedures allows everyone some predictability. It gives form to the dynamics of the workplace. Wow! Be mindful of people's feelings and presumably how you liked or disliked being treated as an employee. Then, go from there. The danger in not establishing boundaries it is that anarchy can be just around the corner.

Here are some boundary examples:

- Our work day will start with a ten minute meeting.
- Personal long distance telephone calls can be made using your credit card.

- Employees will work alternate statutory holidays.

In a world *without* boundaries we would all be bumping into one another!

TRIAL BALANCE

This is an accounting term.

Some balances should be on trial.

The real definition of this term is a list of the debit and credit balances of the accounts in the company's business ledger.

ASSET

This is a corporate term.

In reality, it is anything of value owned by the company.

JOB

This is something we all must have.

The word career comes from French word, "carriere." This French word means highway or its ancient derivation in Sanskrit, "acaria", which means heart. A career is your calling. Most of us really want the career and many of are trying to find our heart. *We all need a job*. Everyone on planet earth has to find a job to pay the bills. Many of us simply *fall* into the jobs we have. All of us need to search out that which we love to do or what we were meant to do.

JUGGLING

An activity that allows us to be called an acrobat.

This is something we all do. Think of the juggler. Watch how he or she balances the items that they juggle. We are all jugglers. We juggle our lives and everything that is in them. Think of the juggler's balls as your personal relationships, your relationship with money and all the paraphernalia that goes along with day-to-day living, children, hobbies, pets, your past, your future, your everything. Imagine them all being in the air at the same time. Sometimes they are.

ZIGGURAT

This is an ancient word.

This word describes a triangular shape or pyramid-like mound found in ancient Sumer. The ziggurat was a temple to the moon and a burial mound for the populace of the city. This civilization based it's economy on the ancient philosophy of the market. It could be the oldest repository of small business artifacts in the world. In fact, there is an archeological legend that this is where the first pyramid sales were invented.

A SLICE OF LIFE

All of these people have the same story with different chapters. Here are some stories that portray the humanity of small business. This is...

A SLICE OF LIFE

What is a mom and pop business?

Look around you!

You have the convenience store, the bakery, the florist, the gas station, the garden centre, the restaurant, the photo shop, the copy shop, the coffee shop. These are the Mom and Pop businesses.

They have nurtured generations of themselves and us. They know our stories and us and we know theirs. In every neighbourhood, they exist. Successive waves of immigration have yielded national 'marketeers'. So you have:

- The Dutch bakery;
- British fish and chips;
- Italian hairdressers;
- Greek and virtually every other nationality of restaurateurs;
- The Ukrainian doctor;
- The carpenters of every nation.

Think of the people in your own neighborhood who run the Chinese restaurant. Think of the people who run the 24-hr. convenience store.

- Who is your hairdresser?
- What family operates the gas station?
- What about the local coffee shop?
- Who is your pharmacist?

OUR LADY OF THE MELON

Once upon a time,

sometime in the early 1960's, there was a convenience store owned by a charming family. The O'Malleys had recently arrived from Ireland. This was at the start of the era of convenience stores.

Couple that with the end of an era of home milk and bread delivery and this convenience store was always full! There were regular lines of people buying staples like bread and milk all the time.

The family drama was played out behind the cash register. The novel and lilting sounds of an Irish inflection were constantly wooing the customers, *"Come on m'darlin' now try some of this."*

The woman's name was Kathleen. She was the family's mother and unbeknownst to her was one of the first exponents of 'the add-on sale'. In the small produce section, this Irish sweetheart said to the constant lineupee, *"Well, now how do you tell whether a cantaloupe is fresh???"* An unsuspecting lineupee, Mrs. Tipples (a woman with glasses) said, *"I don't know."*

Kathleen, that Irish lass, grasped the melon in her two hands and holding the fruit in front of both her face and the face of Mrs. Tipples, said; *"just squeeeeeze"* (almost singing now) and in front of the ever-present line up all the fruit shot out of the melon! The fruit catapulted all over the face and glasses of Mrs. Tipples!!!! This unsuspecting woman had pulp, pith, slush, mush, and seeds dripping, flowing and oozing all over her face. Her earrings, glasses and chins had strands of fleshy, flustered, orange fruit careening off the crags of her kisser. First there was shock! Then you could do nothing but laugh and laugh and laugh. The young son of Mrs. Tipples was howling like the Irish banshee he wasn't. He roared with such joy, that he almost convulsed due to lack of air.

This was one of the most hysterical real life events ever witnessed in that or any other store.

The woman with the glasses became known as our lady of the melon. She subsequently wore a lot of light orange clothing to go with the nickname, and the legend got bigger and bigger, every time it was retold. It became an urban legend.

The whole neighbourhood sighed when in mid-lineup the mother's shift ended and another family member took over. The others just weren't as much fun.

Over the years, we saw the children finish high school, become doctors, and lawyers, and all were married. Friends minded the store on those great occasions.

The youngest child grew up not having to work hard. He was arrogant and rude to the people who had been the family friends and customers for a generation. Because he was the baby he was always exempt from the hard work. All he had to be was cute. As the family money increased he didn't have to slog milk cases, pack the bread aisle, or trim the produce there was staff for that now.

When the father died, the whole area mourned and grieved. The funeral service was held in the local funeral parlour. Whole groups of people sent flowers and signed them from the neighbours. That was the first multi-cultural coming together in that area. Jews, Catholics, Presbyterians, and Anglicans lumped themselves together with their street affiliate and expressed their honest sorrow. The floral tributes poured in. Some inventive neighbourhood florist even found bells of Ireland, that distinctive green bell-shaped flower. While another florist sent an Irish tribute with orange and white roses mixed with the greens it parodied the Irish flag. The school classes of all the children were reunited briefly. They all played the game "catch up on your life" at the funeral parlour. In a tribute to the father the store remained open during the funeral service and then the whole neighbourhood came together at the store with the family they had come to know and love. That Irish family had made a dent on the entire community. They risked their own family story and shared the stories of all their customers. It is a tribute to their zeal and courage that those remaining in that neighbourhood, still remember when the store belonged to them

ADOPTING THE NEIGHBOURHOOD

This is a strategy more retailers should try.

Once upon a time,

just recently there was a well-to-do neighbourhood peppered with convenience stores, kiosks, malls, gas station/food stores, literally places everywhere! There was a poorly-run, dilapidated convenience store next to a liquor store. A young man and his sister bought the store.

First, they cleaned it up. Then, they were nice.

She had a concern and capability far beyond her years. Her name was Mary Ellen. He was hilarious. His name was Ken. Their motto was 'never being able to do enough for you.'

She was beautiful, he was vivacious.

They canvassed the needs of their customer. They talked to the seniors who lived in a nearby home. The seniors wanted English candies. The teenagers requested a line of comics. They changed their product lines. They always encouraged groups of total strangers to buy group lottery numbers. Guess what those people won!!!

Once, when a 'scooterized' senior wandered into the store in a crowd of people, something happened. Woody, an elderly gentleman, was a war veteran. He began to look quizzically around. He was obviously disoriented.

Looking at Ken, Woody barked gruffly, *"What floor is this?"* I've never been on this floor!!! Without missing a beat, Ken said, *"you must have pressed concourse on the elevator."* He then vaulted over the counter and asked an astonished woman to watch the store as he whisked the confused escapee from the senior's home across the parking lot to relative safety within the confines of the senior sanctuary. Another urban legend was born.

These two young entrepreneurs endeared themselves to the crowd of people who flocked daily to the liquor store. They began to carry olives and sour onions (remember they were next to the liquor store) for martinis and gibsons. There was always a special on maraschino cherries for manhattans. Lemons and limes were brought in for gin and tonics and Corona beer. They advertised them as perfect companions. Sales soared!! There was always a special on chips and dip and tacos and salsa to open up the four o'clock cocktail hour. They were now stocking bulk peanuts, nuts and bolts, cashews, and their ever-changing Ken and Mary Ellen mix! They also had free samples of these items on Thursdays and Fridays, which were of course the harbingers of the weekends. They created Tuesdays as Senior's Day and sampled biscuits and herb teas. Once a month when the moon was full they sampled mini chocolate bars for the teen and kid crowd. They didn't just stop there. Cookies and milk were teamed up as were biscuits and tea, wieners and brown beans, French bread and Camembert cheese. This was their natural go-together line. They became competition to the grocery store.

In adopting their neighbourhood, they bought a puppy. I mean how many things are cuter than a puppy? The answer to that question is: nothing, other than your own children. It was hook enough to get even more people through their doors, all of whom bought something. They shared their puppy, their lives and, in return, turned that store into a thriving Mecca of neighbourhood commerce.

MEMORIES

You will always remember some things, like idiosyncratic behaviour from those behind the counters

Once upon a time,

there was a Jewish family who owned the local deli. Theirs was a store chock-a-block full of every conceivable sort of item. Meats, corned beef, kishke, gefilte fish, horseradish, pickled onions, pickled beets, dill pickles, mustard, poupon (before it was fashionable), lox, bagels, buns, rye bread, caraway rye bread, yogurt (before it was everywhere), cheeses, black breads, brandied cherries, havla, chocolate, oil, extra virgin oil. How was that possible? Invariably, Tizzy (that was his name) or his wife Ruth would ask the question, *"Do you want that sliced?"*

Did you hear that? s l i c e d with the accent on the 's l i.'

Everyone in that store got asked that question.

Once they were so busy trying to over-help the Saturday rush that they double sliced a customer!!! That's right, both Tizzy and Ruth asked if Mr. Lempke wanted it sliced! The mirth was infectious.

This couple and their daughter, Hanna (with the scarf tied around her hair) did everything. They went to the market early in the morning. It was 4:30 am early. They huffed and puffed over sacks of onions and bushels of seasonal fruit. They lugged the slabs of deli meats and cheeses, carted the crates of breads and baskets of buns. They unloaded and slugged the jars of mustard. *"Do you vant thet hawt mustarwd?"* There was pickled everything and boxes of Yiddish delicacies. They always had buckets of seasonal flowers to brighten the place up and to make *"another leeetle sale"*. In the days before it was trendy, they made their own herbed vinegars, bottled borscht - even preserved their own garden vegetables. There was always soup and fresh something or other wafting scents of caring throughout the store.

The conversations went something like this:

Mrs. Bittle: *"I'd like a half a pound of corned beef."*

Ruth: *"Do you vant that sliced? Oh, I'm a bit over that, alright?"*

Mrs. Bittle: *"Sure, fine and a half a pound of bologna."*

Ruth: *"Do you vant that sliced? Oh, I'm a bit over that alright?"*

Mrs. Bittle: *"Sure, fine, and a loaf of pumpernickel and five caramel custard squares."*

Ruth would say: *"Do you vant that sliced? The custards, they come in slices of six, that alright?"*

Mrs. Bittle: *"Sure, fine."*

I often wonder if people like Tizzy and Ruth wrote a marketing book what it would look like.

Their life was their customers. Providing their *raison d'etre*. These people nurtured the souls of their customers as well as their stomachs. They stroked the egos of their audiences. As well, they were the play the people came to watch. Theirs was a richly woven fabric that warmed all who knew them.

LIFE & ART

Does life imitate art or does art imitate life??

Once upon a time,

during the last eight years a neighbourhood witnessed a convenience store run by a congenial and much respected man from India. His name was Ashore.

He kept the store scrupulously clean. The items for sale literally shone. I once asked him, *"How is it possible that everything looks so good here?"* He said, *"Oh, very good, thank you. I am putting the higher wattage of bulb in the lights. It is a very good surprise."*

He was always ready. *"Oh how are you today sir?"* and to my son, *"Oh and how are you today, young sir?"*

Once when asked by a patron, *"how are you today,"* Ashore responded in that much-parodied sing-song, *"Ohooooo, verrry goood I am not...my squishy machine, she is broken...."*

The 'Apoo' character from the TV series, 'The Simpsons' was alive and well and living in a suburban convenience store. His kindness was unlimited. This fact, combined with his strict regimen in running the best store in the area garnered him scores of followers. The teens flocked to the store, to buy something, but also to go to that specific store. After all, it had the squishy machine, the popular magazines, and the candy bars, but it also had **the man** behind the counter. They loved to buy from Ashore himself.

The Simpson legend did much to boost his popularity and now, both in and out of the store he is affectionately known as, and called Apoo.

WORK ETHIC

This concept means different things to different nationalities.

I was once asked what nationality I was. Responding that I was Canadian, the question was put to me again,

"Where do your parents come from?"

"They too came from Canada."

"...and their parents???"

"Well, they came from the U.S. and from England." That was an even more bizarre answer and the questioner then looked me in the face and said, *"Awwwchh, but I've never known a Caaanadaian to work."* The questioner was a Dutch woman. It is often said that if you are not Dutch, you're not much!!!!

FAMILY BUSINESS AND THE FAMILY

People who grow up in a family business know it is we versus them.

Once upon a time,

there was a matriarchal woman, who was a hybrid between Broom Hilda and the last Empress of China. Her husband came to Canada with a garden hoe and initially traveled the Hamilton bus lines doing gardening for the well-to-do. The mother started selling plants, perennials and annuals and other gardening paraphernalia from the house. Eventually, as the family expanded, so too did the business. The work ethic was woven into the personalities of the children.

Work, work, work, both in school and out of school. They went to horticultural college and worked on the weekends. The business now had grown *unbelieeveably*. The garden centre had become a hub in the spring for plant enthusiasts trying to recreate Victoria in the backyards of Burlington. The family grew and you guessed it. Their drama was played out every spring for their customers and themselves.

For ninety days their business was a sitcom to rival *Coronation Street*. These people worked ten to fifteen hours a day non-stop. They expected the same of their employees. They lived on the site and wondered why people couldn't be on time for the 7:00 a.m. opening. Primarily, the staff didn't have the luxury of just falling out of bed and being in their place of employment. The same situation occurred at the end of the day. 5:30 p.m. rolled around and the staff made their way home via public transit, walking, hitchhiking, or by car. The family walked into the house to dinner on the table at 5:45 p.m.

Customers and staff alike watched as the competing egos jockeyed for position and for dominance in an ever-expanding and successful business operation. The mother never lost the Broom Hilda look. She still used the techniques of the harridan of Hertogenbosch as she *screeeamed* for her son or daughter to attend her and do it now.

As the business grew it sprawled itself over a 29-acre sales site. Think of that, a 29-acre sales site is larger than most medium-sized shopping malls.

Initially the mother and the father could control things by simply using the most effective form of communication, YELLING. As technology was added, first an intercom, then expanded phone support and then two-way radios, the intention was to bypass the first line of their historic method of communication. **Not so**, every family member continued to yell into each new device of communication. It was comical beyond belief and yet they couldn't see the comedy because they *were* it!

The strain on the family was horrific. They were a business that grew way out of proportion with their capabilities. It was hard work. They had to make their money in ninety days of spring torture. They also had to remain a family. The anger, frustration, and mistrust of those who constantly let them down were due, in part, to the unrealistic expectations placed on both themselves and their employees. It was ever-present in their dealings with the public, themselves, and their staff.

It was a family and a business out of control.

Early one Saturday morning, Giancomo, an elderly Italian man approached the aging mother, Johanna and said,

"This a tree, she's a dead."

The offending arbor was a plum tree purchased the spring before. The mother, now known affectionately to her staff as old Buddha, barely looked up and said in her stage whisper:

"Awwwch tooo deeeep planted."

This whole drama was being unwittingly played out over the telephone intercom, left on by her son who was too hung-over that morning to remember to turn it off.

The man sighed and reiterated, *"she's a dead"*. He flung the tree at the woman, who had refused to look at him as he screamed, *"you are a robber."* Hardly missing a beat in her role as dominatrix of the garden centre, Johanna grabbed the tree and hurled it back to him screeching, that he was full of rubbish.

Then something happened.

Both caught the eye of each other and they began to laugh. They laughed and laughed. Both these elderly people, not wanting to give in, realized the hilarity of the situation. He got a new tree. She got a friend. They often shared Saturday morning coffee together.

THE DEDICATED EMPLOYEE

We have all started out as an employee.

Once upon a time,

we have all worked for someone else at one time or another. So how did we measure up? Were we late? What is late anyway?

In school, late is anytime after the bell rings. Most school children and certainly the teaching community know the value and importance of nine o'clock.

But in the workplace???

Let us assume the start time is nine o'clock. Should the employee be walking in the door at nine or starting to work at nine?

If the employee walks in the door at nine then he or she actually has to get their outerwear off. Then the next item is to prepare his or her desk, bench, or sales station. Then we need to get ready to perform the opening daily routine. How long does that take? What time is it now? Are you late yet?

How about the employee who comes in with coffee in hand? This person then proceeds to drink that caffeine beverage during the opening part of the day. Usually this type of employee is the one who asks for their coffee break first.

Point of Interest

During an eight-hour workday the employee is not entitled to any coffee breaks. They are, however, entitled to a half-hour unpaid lunch break.

How about the employee who waltzes in at the stroke of nine and:

- spends 10 to 12 minutes in the staff bathroom remaking themselves;
- waltzes out onto the floor and proceeds to busy themselves with making or getting coffee/tea or whatever;
- fusses over their workstation, etc.;
- Presto! It's 9:30 am and this person is just starting to work.

Now is this person late?

Pity the poor employer who criticizes the employee for being late. What is late anyway?

In the above instance that person would look at you transfixed and say: *"Well, I was here at nine!"*

In suggesting that the employee come in ten to fifteen minutes before start time the retort is:

"Am I going to be paid for the quarter of an hour before nine?"

"No," is the answer.

There are employees who will in fact come to work that extra early time only to spend it socializing outside the place of employment and then casually amble in and start on the stroke of nine!

IRREPLACEABLE

Remember no one is irreplaceable.

Once upon a time,

there was once an employee who expostulated that he was the greatest thing since sliced bread to this company. He knew everything about every dimension of this entire field. It was his fifth career path. Jorgen was always late! A few minutes here or there. Even the nine o'clock strutters were in place and fussing ABOUT and ACTUALLY GETTING DOWN TO WORK. Jorgen the drama queen would waltz in and then incredulously sit down and eat! Sometimes shilly-shallying over to co-workers with morsels of what he was knoshing. Not everyone, mind you. Only when he was sated would he fidget over putting things away and get down to do his indispensable work. The lesson this person needed to learn was nobody is irreplaceable.

Then, there are the people who have legitimate late excuses. They are always apologetic, get right to their work, and often as not, attempt to make up the missed time. Take the indispensable (or so they thought) clerk who took his work home every night. The next morning he could be seen lugging the work to the car, and eventually in from the parking lot to the work station. It looked to all the world, employees and outsiders alike, that this person was loyal, a workaholic and dedicated. That was the idea. Whenever the supervisor was away, this individual was socializing, gabbing, talking, and having coffee. The work remained undone due to the time spent away from work.

It is a sad statistic that most Canadians work only 20 minutes out of every hour. Stated another way, Canadians work one out of every three minutes.

GO AHEAD TRY IT! TEST YOURSELF AND YOUR STAFF, SEE HOW MANY MINUTES PER HOUR YOU AND THEY ACTUALLY WORK.

In a place of employment, where there is a time clock you are late and docked 15 minutes if you are one minute past the designated start time. Similarly you are docked for time infractions as they occur exponentially in that system.

This is a system not many small businesses have in place. The time card or the sophisticated swipe card should be implemented. All of these systems have employer and employee boundary wars. Why is it that the employer always wants to talk to the employee after they clock out?

WORKPLACE DEMEANOR

This is the warp and weft of human life.

Once upon a time,

you have all been in the work environment where there are three people, you know the Jack, Kathy and Mary of any workplace. These people are your colleagues sometimes your friends. It is here that you find the warp and weft of human life. There are so many stories that occur that often the fabric of life becomes mixed up with the material of work? Where do you draw the line?

Should you draw the line with the employee John whose wife is dying? The woman has contracted a terminal illness and is forced to leave her job. John was paralyzed at work. Sympathy and pathos abound for the man at work. His work day was played out around the events of the hospital and the quickly dying wife. His day involved visiting on the way into work, a longer lunch hour to accommodate another visit, and then a prolonged visit on the way home. Any suggestion that the man take a leave of absence to be with the dying individual is met with the hurt expostulation *"How could I leave my work?"* or, *"I can't afford not to work, I need the money."*

Meanwhile, the work that he was doing is suffering in quality and quantity. When the end ultimately comes, the staff do the requisite floral tribute, a delegation is sent to the funeral and the man is encouraged to take some time to mourn in private. This he does and disappears to a family member somewhere in the middle of the United States of America. After not hearing from this person for well over seven weeks, the workplace people are becoming concerned. Finding John's children was an investigative piece of work, and when asked about his absence they said,

"Dad would be in touch."

It was a shocked John who phoned and said,

"Well, you said take as much time as you wanted."

The requisite amount of time off at a death is *three* days.

The grieving man returns to work and now in the drama of the workplace, recounts to all who would listen the events of the dying and the death, the funeral and the time in the United States. He recounts how the American part of the family had encouraged him to become a member of their family business with much of the proceeds from the insurance policy. Thank goodness for the house being life insured and how he doesn't really have to work but how could he give up his work, it was everything to him. Every new anniversary was a crisis, and all the stories would come out again. The customers and all around were living the story and trying to be supportive. When counselling was suggested once again it was met with disbelief. About eighteen months later, the requisite time for healing from grief had passed this man moved on to another job wondering how he could have remained in a dead end job for so long.

WOULD YOU BELIEVE...OR 'WHY I CAN'T COME TO WORK' STORIES

Once upon a time,

we have all been either the employee or the employer. We have all had the staff or collegial chat of where is Joe today? Some of us have experienced some of these tales. These anecdotes could make great sitcoms. They could have even rivaled 'Seinfeld.'

Here are some goodies:

- The woman who is always complaining about work place conditions, from the boss, to the new employees on down to the work and anything in general. She meanders into the baking area of her place of employment. She drops a tart shell on the floor and inadvertently slips and falls loudly on the floor. This woman worked that slip into a seven month paid leave of absence and a chronic complaint with periodic bouts of leave for the next five years of her employment.

- The man who calls at 10:00 am on behalf of his wife who was supposed to be in work at 8:30 and says to the employer, *"Ugh, last night my wife died,"* and just leaves it there. The thunderstruck and unprepared employer says, *"Well, does that mean she isn't coming to work?"*

- The secretary who calls her boss and says she's not feeling well, and then literally bumps into her boss's daughter while shopping.

- The woman who has the 26 oz flu. She calls in and says she can't make it to work, only to have her parents drop in at noon to pick her up as per her request for lunch. She neglected to tell her parents that she was not at work.

- Johan was a schemer. He spent more time coming up with inventive ways around work than actually working. Once, he went to the trouble of having a fake body cast put on. He claimed that he couldn't come to work for six weeks. It was just after the company shut for the two week paid Christmas vacation. After the supervisor visited him at home, he was put on short-term disability. The work schedule and workloads were re-arranged to accommodate his absence. His colleagues shouldered the brunt of his work. In reality, he was in Whistler skiing, and through a clever hookup of call forwarding and messaging, he kept in touch with work, and basically had eight weeks paid holiday at the expense of his boss and co-workers.

- All right, you have all heard about the worker who has had the flu, a cold or maybe even a chronic headache. How about the person who went outside the place of employment, and went home?! When asked why, the answer was, *"well I took a deep breath and cracked one of my ribs."*

- You have all heard of the employee who works here but also has something on the side. You know the fireman who is a plumber, the teacher who is a landscaper, the bank teller who is a caterer, or the person who also does flowers on the side. Well you bet, the flower person calls in sick one day and says,

"I can't come in for the next three days." Coincidentally it was wedding season. Fittingly enough the well-meaning co-workers get together to send flowers to the ailing individual. Think of the poor unfortunate who had to make the call to the local florist. The person who answered the phone at the florist was none other than his co-worker to whom they were sending flowers!

WANTED

Loyal individual who is prepared to put in long hours, who has intimate knowledge of the family business, who knows the secrets of the employees, who will work for more money than his co-workers.

If you come to a small family business, this vacancy will be filled by the son or daughter of the owner. Employees know the family members of the boss as 'rellis' which is short for relative. Yes, workers of small businesses know all about this.

The little Petey, Joey, Joany and Vita that you cooed over in the early stages of their young life will be coming to a place of employment near you. In fact, they will work beside you. That cute little so and so that you watched grow up will now become your co-worker and eventually your boss.

When little Mario or Mary, is now on the floor beside you, it changes the whole workplace dynamics. The employee now gets to have the role of on the job trainer. Lo and behold, the trainee is the son, daughter, cousin, niece, or nephew of the boss. When the workday is done and you go home to your family and whine about the day's events, you must understand that so does the young apprentice.

You are now cast in the starring role of all the day's stories as either villain or hero and sometimes both!

It looks a little different when the rummy relatives are at work. Suddenly there is money for lunch, and little extras. Remember the fleet of vehicles that the company owns? You have been keeping your vehicle neat as a pin for years. You had hoped to get the new truck when it came. Lo and behold the new truck goes to the 'relli' (see definition on page 99). Not only that, the relli keeps the truck like a pigsty and you end up cleaning up after the kid returns to school on Mondays. It is the exceptional boss who introduces the son or daughter with appropriate boundaries and safety checks to enshrine the existing dynamics of the employees or team of workers.

In reality, it is hard on the child of the boss, the boss, and the workers. Usually the son or daughter doesn't really want to be there. Sometimes they want to play. Goodness knows they were encouraged to play or keep themselves busy when they were too young to actually work. The boss is usually on edge because he wants his offspring to appear as near perfect as possible. They aren't. The least little infraction on behalf of the unsuspecting progeny is met with huge overreaction. The expectation that this kid can do no wrong is totally inappropriate. The learning curve for both the parent and child is always accelerated, but yet the learning time is always too late.

The feelings of the workers are always on edge. Suddenly things that have been acceptable for years are called into question.

"That's not the way we do things here", is the all too often-heard expression when for years that is exactly how things were done. Who amongst us has the audacity to correct the parent in front of the child at the workplace?

And what if you and the relative don't get along???

RELATIVE WORKER STORY #309

Once upon a time,

Uta applied for a job. She is the youngest sister of the wife of the son who is now managing director. She has some credentials for this position. Not a lot, but some. She also has worked for a major competitor. There were others more suited for this spot. The personnel manager was caught in a bind. The department head didn't like Uta. This was discussed with the family and on the way out one night the wife of the son looked at the personnel manager and said *"Well you know family is family."* The next day Uta was on board.

Uta became everyone's nightmare. Her work was shoddy. She had an opinion on everything. You would hear this is how so and so did it at the competition. Her opinion sounded like the opinions of her sister. She was currently living with her sister in one of their spare rooms until she could find her own place. She missed appointments, she argued with her department head, and then she went home with the boss. The tension intensified. She should have been fired for the first twelve infractions. Others would have been gone after three. Finally it comes down to she goes or we lose the department head. She is at last moved to another area. This was seemingly a promotion. She finally returned, back to the competition as she had lost her primary audience.

RELATIVE WORKER STORY #310

Or how about the daughter, Zelda, who is the youngest of the owner's children and is retained in the family business when it is sold. This person loses her status as 'the owner's daughter.' The new owners have children of their own.

The former owner's daughter is now in a state of flux. Her parents had given her power way beyond her age and ability. She, like many owner's children treated the employees more like serfs than people. It was when she finally overstepped her boundaries once too often that she realized she was an employee just like everyone else, and that things had changed

THE RELLIS ARE COMING!

(see relli in the glossary)

"Why are we cleaning continually this week?"

"Didn't you know? The owner's parents are coming for a visit!!!"

Wow! Here's what happens when Baba, Seda, Gran, Gramma, BAMA, Boom Boom, or whatever the owners of your establishment call their parents, grandparents, aunts, uncles, or siblings are en route. *Everyone* knows they are coming for a visit.

The premises are painted, the stock polished, the detail is unbelievable. Windows, walls, washrooms and whatnots are scrubbed, scraped, and skewered within an inch of their life. Vacuuming takes on a new meaning.

Paperwork is brought up to date, work schedules are re-arranged to accommodate the nothing less than state visit status that these occasions engender. The owners go through the gyrations of an acrobatic tightrope walker, as their children are cleaned and polished. Their houses and the grounds are turned into a park-like state for the inspection of the unsuspecting relative review. The city itself in which the business is located is virtually put on alert and all the best parts of the city are the now the only routes on which the visiting party may travel. Restaurants are gone over and the larder is stocked with the holiday treats as if they were indeed everyday items.

When the magic moment is actually at hand and the almost regal relatives are escorted into the now sparkling spot of commerce, it is indeed all too much like a royal walk about. The staff are trotted out like the retainers they're not. They all meet and greet the family scions, while bobbing and accepting outstretched limbs as if they were made of gold or other precious metals. Meanwhile, the rellis try to put the right name, face and stories of the year to the proper individual.

Everyone tries to get the most memorable word in so that the employees can have a nice thing to say about the relatives and also the Baba, Gramma, Zeda person can remember the correct story about the employee whom their son or daughter has told them so much about.

Usually the employee who is the least memorable and does the least amount of work is remembered by the family visitors as, *"Isn't that a nice person, dear."*

Everyone needs time off after they have left. Lethargy takes about a week to work itself back into the family business.

COFFEE STORES, COFFEE SHOPS, CARTS AND COFFEE KIOSKS

The family drama continues as in the drama in the local coffee/muffin place.

Coffee places have become the gold mines of the late nineties. Take the story of the middle European family who buys the local coffee and muffin eatery. They barely speak English. There is Misha the father, three girls whose names are Anna, Tanya, and Gloria and a son named Sasha.

They don't have the same allure as the former owners. No new owners ever have the same allure as the former proprietor. It is just an owner thing. Misha the dad is a great cook. He introduces such new menu items as cabbage rolls, and different breads and new desserts. These are menu selections that the regulars are not used to. The girls give great service, and now the little restaurant is filled up with more than just the regulars. They add some decor touches. The restaurant now has a lineup for lunch and is jammed at breakfast. The adjustment period for the neighbourhood is about thirteen months, but occasionally you still hear that the old owner never did it that way - rings true doesn't it?

THE CUSTOMER IS ALWAYS RIGHT

Remember the old maxim, *"the customer is always right?"*

Well, the fact is that the customer always *thinks* that they are right. They want to be appeased. They want to be coddled, cuddled and cosseted and made to feel all better. Many times, they are completely…**WRONG!**

The merchant class has bought into that old sentiment, hook, line and sinker.

Here are some stories with a strikingly familiar ring of truth to them.

THE FREQUENT SHOPPER

Once upon a time,

a customer enters into a store that has just transferred ownership. It is a dry goods store with a number of departments. The customer, Ned, is a senior citizen, and a longtime patron of the store. One of the departments in this store is hardware. Ned comes in and looks for the former owner. He asks for the owner by name.

"Is Tom around?"

"No", he is told that Tom is no longer the owner here and the new owner's name is Jack. *"Could I help you?"* Jack asks.

The store is deathly quiet. There are a few customers and about five former staff. Everyone has instantly tuned into Ned.

"Well, three years ago I bought these two items." Out of a crumpled and gnarled, brown paper bag, Ned gingerly removes two shrink-wrapped ceiling plugs for a hanging planter. Ned places them on the table. The total dollar value for these items amounts to $11.39.

Looking Jack straight in the eye he says,
"I bought these three years ago here at this store and I don't want them anymore. I am moving now, and I would like my money back."

The silence could not have been any louder.

Jack knew the ice he was on was thin. He asks, *"when did you buy these items, sir?"*

"Well, three years ago and I haven't opened them and here is my receipt and I would like my money back!"

Jack could hear the ice cracking as he said,

"Well I'm very sorry sir, but I can't refund money from three years ago."

Ned the, elderly gentleman is now vexed, perplexed, and mad as well. He declares, in a loud, quivering voice for all to hear, *"Tom would have given me my money back. I'll never do business with you again."*

He grabs his three year old unopened items and grumbles his way out of the store never to be heard of or seen again.

Everyone within earshot of that incident had an opinion that day. I'm sure you do too. Write or email who was in the right. Our reader's poll will be published in our sequel!

MY LIFE REVOLVES AROUND ME.

The staff are just completing their end of the day routine. It has been a harrowing day in the small flower shop. Unseasonable snow had fallen making their deliveries treacherous. The world was seeing the horrors of the Bosnia conflict. This town had just seen several hundred of their citizens sent there as peacekeepers. The telephone rings and the voice on the other end requisitions the owner's presence in a rather high handed fashion.

"Good evening, Zachary speaking how may I help you?"

"Are you the owner?" demands Mrs. Highhand. *"Yes, how can I help you?"*

"Well I ordered flowers this morning for a Mrs. Blackbody, and they weren't delivered until late this afternoon."

"Well, just let me check our log book."

In the meantime, the staff are collecting themselves and wondering what this woman is wanting on the phone.

"Mrs. Highhand, I don't see a specific request for this delivery to be made in the morning. The flowers were delivered as ordered even in

the unexpected snow with the treacherous driving conditions. What exactly is the problem?"

"The problem, the problem, you insolent young man (note that nothing insolent has been said to date) is that my friend didn't get to enjoy her birthday flowers on the day of her birthday. I mean, what good is it when the birthday flowers ordered in the morning don't get delivered until the afternoon? I have never been so furious in my life."

"Mrs. Highhand, these flowers were the twelfth order in today and delivered on the day requested, and there were no specific instructions as to a timed delivery. I'm sorry you are upset, but this conversation is over."

The receiver of the phone is returned to the cradle.

The staff are now clustered around the phone, the story is told to the staff and the staff are questioned just to make sure that a verbal request hadn't been missed. The boss is somewhat excited and not a little miffed. The phone rings again. The phone is picked up and the caller hears, *"ABC Florist ,can we help you?"*

"I'd like to speak to the owner".

Zachary replies, *"This is the owner."* in a firm yet steady voice. It is now fifteen minutes past closing and the staff who are all ready to go, stay for the next installment for what is becoming a radio call in show before the invention of such greats as Dr. Laura.

"This is Mrs. Highhand calling and I am still furious about the flowers not being delivered until late this afternoon. I can't believe you hung up on me."

This woman is now using a twenty-three decibel shrill on her end of the telephone. In fact she didn't need the phone. She could have opened her window and the entire city could have listened to her bemoaning the apparent apathetic and unjust inefficiencies of this floral firm. She continued, *"I just can't believe you hung up on me, I just can't...."*

Zachary excused himself and said, *"You can't believe I hung up on you???"* with a great interrogatory intonation. *"Well watch this...."* and he dropped the phone back into its cradle.

The store staff looks on incredulously as the ire of the owner has been piqued to the point of hanging up on the unreasonable woman not once but *twice*!

You can only imagine how this too, became an urban myth in that community. Overheard in the shopping line was the same story and one of the lineupees said to her friend,

"Well, I would have hung up on her twice too!"

WHO'S RIGHT?

In the small everyday life of the florist, the order for a dozen roses is the big sale. When a man calls from his car as he is arriving home from out of town and orders a dozen roses for his wife, the whole store gets in on the act.

What a nice husband, etc. The order is prepared. The extra touches of baby's breath, and a big bow, are added. The roses are carefully placed in water tubes and the instructions for after care placed in the box. The driver goes on his way to make the delivery and returns to give a report of a beautiful big house on a hill.

Monday morning rolls around and the phone rings with a request to speak to the manager. The manager takes the phone and the caller identifies herself as Mrs. Silvershooze. The conversation goes something like this:

"My husband ordered these roses for me on Friday and they are dead."

"I'm sorry to hear that. Did you follow the instructions on the rose card?"

"Of course, I've been receiving roses for years", she says

emphatically.

"Well, that shouldn't happen. Can we send you another dozen to replace those?"

"Yes but not until Thursday. I'm out of town until then" and click goes the receiver.

The manager dutifully logs the event and then casually asks if anyone remembers this person as a regular customer. No, none of the staff does.

The replacement order is sent out as requested on Thursday, no bow no extras. On Saturday afternoon, a large beige Cadillac careens into the parking lot to take up two parking stalls and the handicapped parking spot.

A woman flies into the floral shop with a rumpled reef of roses peeking out of a masticated rose box clutched in her claws. With as much indignity as she can muster, this woman who was dripping in everything silver, (including her Mexican earrings, her silver footgear and matching clutch purse), announces that she is Mrs. Silverschooz and,

"These roses weren't any good either. What are you people going to do about it?"

This query was hurled at anyone who would listen.

The manager looks at the roses, notes that they have not been re-cut as per the instruction sheet and replies, *"Unfortunately, nothing. These roses were not re-cut as per our instructions, and we have already replaced this item once."*

Unclenching the floundering flowers, Mrs. Silvershooz spins around in a sterling, twister-like motion and stomps out, announcing in a withering tone that she and her friends will never darken the doors of this establishment again.

HOW MUCH DID THEY SPEND?

Florists always experience the crush of Mother's Day, Valentines, and Christmas. These are the biggest floral holidays of the year. The effort that these workers go through to meet the needs of their customers are indeed worthy of note. While the goal is to please everyone, that is not always the case. Here are some glimpses of what happens after Mother's Day, Valentine's Day and Christmas.

Phone call #1

"Is the manager there?"

"Yes this is the manager."

"This is Mrs. Madcap calling and I'm complaining about what my son sent me for Mother's Day."

"Just a moment please. Let me get the order." The order being retrieved is for a $15.00 plant. *"Mrs. Madcap, what is the matter with the plant?"*

"Well it is very small. He knows I don't like pink and well I just know he would have spent much more money on me."

So now what do you do? Tell her that her son only spent $15.00 of which $5.00 was delivery?

"Well why don't you call your son and have him call us and we'll see if we can straighten this out."

Phone Call #2

"Is the manager there?"

"This is the manager. Can I help you?"

"Yes, I'm calling to complain about these roses."

"What seems to be the problem?'

"Well, they're dead."

"How long have you had them?"

"Well, let's see now twelve days. When will you replace them?"

"Well, actually we don't replace roses after twelve days. That is excellent value for your money."

Most merchants and businesses go out of their way to endorse community events.

REQUEST #335443

"Hi, we are having this neighbourhood fund raiser. We would like your sponsorship".(read a donation of $50 to $100). *"You would receive lots of free publicity as we are going to raffle off your product."*

Little do these people realize that they are just one of a huge number of people who come in asking for the same thing. That wouldn't be so bad but when the same group of people goes to the competition to buy a lower priced similar article, who is supporting whom?

THE NUTS AND BOLTS

In the neighbourhood automotive shop, the mechanic worked all day to repair an old beater of a car. They reground this and that, and had the car purring like a kitten when the owner returned.

The owner of the car, Danielle (clothed in enough leather to outfit several couches), went up one side of the clerk and down the other side over the cost of the repairs.
"How could this cost so much" and yappity-yap-yap-yap. She was quite annoying. This woman was way off base considering the time and effort in repairing the old parts. The mechanics could have of replaced them with new more costly items. Well, unbeknownst to this woman the owner's wife, Glinda was listening to this diatribe.

She burst upon the scene, grabbed the keys and tore up the work order. Glinda had fire in her eyes and her ocular slits narrowed in feline anger. She spat out, *"Don't like our work or prices? Fine no one goes home until the following is done."* Glinda told her mechanics to undo all their work and to be quick about it. Glinda then gave the keys to the car back to the complainant, with the further instructions to not come back.

So, THIS IS THE END, and it is also the beginning. It is end of the first sequel of *Small Business Sucks*!

This book is dedicated to all of you in whatever country you are living and making a life from small business!

It is a tribute to people who go out of their way to give outstanding service day after day, year-in and year-out, for entire life times, or 24/7/365!

Let some of these pages be a beacon of hope and reinforcement for those of you who are struggling with the nitty-gritty and the mundane. Let some of these pages provide fun and amusement for those of you who might need to lighten up a little.

Let this book also be a beginning as you can interface with SBS (*Small Business Sucks*) by emailing your stories, your thoughts and your words to add to our glossary. We are already working on *Small Business Sucks Part 2*. Look for it! It will be coming to a small business near you! We are also working on the following "sucks" titles or projects concurrently: *banking, government, gardening, teaching* and *taxes, as well as* other titles that will effect a positive change in the social conscience!"

Our email address is sbs@canada.com
...write us today!

ISBN 1-55212-392-8